W9-CDH-800

TEACHING TO INTUITION

Constructive Implementation of the Common Core State Standards in Mathematics

Edric Cane

Also by Edric Cane:

Making Friends with Numbers

For more material, feedback, comments, and to continue the
conversation go to: TeachingtoIntuition.com

© 2013 Edric Cane

All Rights Reserved.

No part of this publication may be reproduced, stored in a
retrieval system, or transmitted, in any form or by any means,
electronic, mechanical, photocopying, recording, or otherwise,
without the written permission of the author.

2

Available in print and electronic formats.

This edition published by
Dog Ear Publishing
4010 W. 86th Street, Ste H
Indianapolis, IN 46268

www.dogearpublishing.net

ISBN: 978-145751-865-2
This book is printed on acid-free paper.

Printed in the United States of America

My thanks to

Frankie Steven

for asking me a seven word question to which I gave a three word answer.

Initially, I thought I had unrelated strategies that students seemed to appreciate. Frankie asked me a question that took me by surprise: *"What do they all have in common?"* A few days later, I had an answer for her and more importantly for me: *"Teaching to intuition."* What these very different strategies on very different topics all had in common was a determined effort to reach a sweet spot in students' understanding that these three words seemed to convey. Frankie is not a math teacher, but the insight I gained by answering her question has helped me become a better teacher.

In *Teaching to Intuition*, I try to present some of those strategies and an understanding of what they have in common.

Contents

Intuition

Intuition is at the heart of mathematics. It is central, for instance, to the abstraction process that gets me from the practical experience of the period at the end of this sentence, a point that grows larger with magnification, to an understanding of a point as a mathematical object, immune to magnification.

Defining *mathematics* in his *Dictionary of Mathematics Terms*, Douglas Downing writes that

> the objects that mathematicians talk about correspond to objects about which we have an intuitive understanding. For instance, we have an intuitive notion of what a number is, what a line in three-dimensional space is, and what probability is.

Intuition is not only present at the foundation of mathematics. It is the bond that justifies my acquiescence to the processes and conclusions of mathematics. As such, it should be central to the learning process. Those "aha" moments that we all see as successful teaching episodes happen when students recognize in what we want to teach an echo of patterns and understandings that are already in their minds. They are a manifestation of intuition at work.

So, from the outset, there is nothing "unmathematical" about intuition. By consciously relying on it, by setting up intuitive knowledge as our highest standard, we are not betraying mathematics. No student is ever shortchanged as we teach to intuition. To the contrary, they may be acquiring the only skill that cannot be fully taken over by computers. More importantly, students embrace the approach and begin to thrive as they discover mathematics as a formulation and extension of their own inner understandings and requirements.

All quotations from the Common Core State Standards (the standards) are from the Content Standards for mathematics, the Standards for Mathematical Practice, or the accompanying introduction and documentation. Authors and Publishers: National Governors Association Center for Best Practices, Council of Chief State School Officers, Washington D.C. Copyright: 2010.

To the Reader

Leaders in education, business, industry, and government are unanimous in seeing in the current situation of math education in the United States an existential threat to the future standing of the nation in a globalized economy. The gap between our needs and reality is reflected in this nation's international ranking, in the shrinking percentage of high-tech and engineering jobs filled by our own graduates, and in the number of remedial classes on elementary and middle school topics given by most community colleges. We have the gap between those who graduate from high school and those who drop out; between zip codes that mean success and those that imply failure; between the excellent quality of much of our advanced teaching on mathematics in high schools and universities and the large pool of students who are just not ready to benefit from that education.

At its heart, the gap is not just a matter of mathematical facts and processes that students don't know. It is an estrangement from mathematics itself. That estrangement by a significant proportion of students and of the adults they become is what *Teaching to Intuition* seeks to address.

Many teachers see in the approach a reflection of their own efforts to reach out to their students' intimate understanding. They find in it an affirmation of their quest for authenticity in what it means to know and understand mathematics. They find in *Teaching to*

Intuition practical approaches that can help them implement the Common Core State Standards' efforts to replace mechanical processing with understanding and to tie more closely the abstractions of mathematics with the real world we want to analyze, model, and influence.

Born of experience, *Teaching to Intuition* seeks to achieve its goals not through abstract statements of principles but through practical, sometimes detailed strategies on specific topics that teachers can immediately use in their classrooms. As they do so, as they adjust the strategies to the specific needs of their students, as they improve on them and expand the approach to topics not discussed here, as they discuss the topics with their colleagues, we urge them to take into account the real purpose of these examples. We want to reconcile students with mathematics itself and invite teachers to look beyond their own classrooms and the grades that they teach, beyond the specific examples that they can borrow, and participate in a recasting of what it means to know math in a way that will broaden its appeal to all students.

Though teaching to our students' intuitive understanding can be applied at higher levels, in *Teaching to Intuition* we focus on elementary and middle school mathematics. It is at that early stage that the gaps begin and ripple up along the grades. That is where too many children lose ground and lose hope, and where real progress can be achieved at the least cost.

That is also where a significantly greater proportion of students able and eager to embrace the challenges of a society molded by science and technology can prepare to fill gaps that lie far beyond those early years.

At the Checkout Counter

Let's look together at a line of people at the checkout counter of a supermarket. It may seem surprising at first sight, but no one seems to panic as they approach the salesclerk! No one even seems to fret! They have no worry at all about the order in which their purchases are scanned or whether their discount coupons are scanned each after the discounted item or all together at the end or somewhere in between. They understand that it doesn't make any difference if they pay for the sandwiches and the chicken wings at the deli and for the prescriptions at the pharmacy instead of paying for everything at the checkout counter along with their other purchases. This lady is leaving the checkout counter. Let's ask her a few questions.

Me: So your name is Mary. You seem to clip coupons quite efficiently. How much did you save today with those coupons?

Mary: Let's see. I had a $2.00 coupon on a pound of cheese and three $1.00 coupons on soft drinks. I saved $5.00. No, more than that. My sales slip reminds me here that I had a $3.00 coupon on a box of cereal. I also used a $2.00 coupon at the pharmacy on some vitamins that I bought along with my prescriptions. In all, I saved $10.00.

My coupons are paying for this nice big piece of meat.

Me: Congratulations. I seem to remember that the second item you scanned was a jar of pickles. I saw you give it back at the end. Why did you change your mind?

Mary: I just had two twenty-dollar bills. I didn't want to spend more than $40.00. At the end, I noticed my bill was going to be almost $43.00. So I handed back that $4.00 jar of pickles. See, I just had to pay $38.95.

Me: Thank you, Mary. You've been very helpful.

The scene and the imaginary conversation demonstrate a good amount of mathematical understanding on the part of those shoppers. We all agree, I guess, that it is intuitive knowledge, not the result of math classes. If the shoppers don't panic as they stand in line, it is not because they suddenly remember that the commutative property of addition tells them that the total cost of their purchases is not affected by the order in which their items are scanned. They don't need deep reflections on grouping to make the choice of paying their deli purchases at the deli or at the checkout counter. In fact, those shoppers know more than the commutative and associative properties could teach them, as these apply to addition only, not subtraction.

Focusing on these shoppers helps us stare intuitive mathematical knowledge in the eyes and convinces us of its concrete, practical reality. We can then ask ourselves how, on this and on entirely different topics, we can ground our teaching strategies on establishing a strong connection between that preexisting knowledge and the topics we want our students to learn. This may imply not just a recasting of the topics but a different understanding of what it means to know. The Common Core State Standards seek to be an antidote to knowledge that is "a mile wide and an inch deep." We hope *Teaching to Intuition* can make a contribution to that vitally important goal.

At the heart of the intuitive understanding demonstrated by Mary and the other shoppers, there is this simple insight:

> A $4.00 box of cereal adds $4.00 to my total bill. A $1.00 discount coupon reduces my total bill by $1.00. This remains true whether the box is scanned at the beginning, in the middle, or at the end or whether the discount coupon is scanned immediately after the discounted item or at any other time.

These are assumptions that are made as the $4.00 box is pulled from the shelf and tossed into the shopping cart or as the $1.00 coupon is being clipped.

As a related conviction, there is this understanding:

> It doesn't make any difference if I pay all my deli purchases in one group at the deli or if I scatter them among my other purchases at the check out counter: a $5.00 sandwich still adds $5.00 to my final cost, and a $2.00 discount

coupon still reduces my final out of pocket expense by $2.00.

This is clear to these shoppers:

A $10.00 savings somewhere or scattered throughout can be used to balance off and pay for a $10.00 expense somewhere else.

That is already a lot of knowledge bearing one way or another on the order of operations. If we invited Mary for a cup of coffee, I'm sure we could discover that she knows that we need to multiply before we can add or subtract. The conversation might take place as follows:

Me: I see you bought 10 cans of peas at $0.75 each. Did the salesclerk scan them each separately?

Mary: No. She only scanned one. I told her I had 10. She trusted me and she typed "10" in her machine.

Me: Do you mean that she added 10 to your total bill?

Mary: No, of course not. That's just the number of cans. See, the tape shows $7.50, the cost of my 10 cans.

Me: So the machine changed 10 cans at $0.75 into a total cost of $7.50 and added that amount to your bill?

Mary: Isn't that obvious?

By the way, what do you do for a living? You teach math, don't you?

Any more probing on my part and I would appear as a complete idiot. Maybe it was too late already.

Clearly, Mary knew that you can only add dollars to her total bill, not the number of cans. She knew that you need to multiply the cost of a can by the number of cans, in the process translating the two numbers into a single dollar amount. Only then can you add that dollar amount to the other dollar amounts. She may never have thought about it before, but somehow, somewhere she knew that we need to multiply before adding or subtracting. How many among our students have any idea why multiplication and division must be done before addition and subtraction? They know it as a rule of mathematics. They have no understanding of why it must be so. As shoppers, they would know. We can help them establish a connection between two levels of knowledge. In particular, on this as on other topics, numbers attached to things can throw a light that remains invisible when rules and procedures are used with numbers in the abstract.

So there is a considerable amount of mathematical knowledge among these shoppers. It is knowledge that comes from being rational human beings, endowed with common sense, able to live, drive, marry, raise kids, and think. If it was knowledge learned in school, we can imagine that there would be a few among all those shoppers that had not mastered the topic. It has probably never been formulated or recognized by them, but it is there nevertheless. It is intuitive knowledge, and we wanted to take a good look at it right from the start.

> Teaching to our students' intuition means helping them, whenever possible, recognize in mathematics an echo of truths and of mental structures that are already theirs. This allows them to give their willing allegiance to the truths of mathematics and to see the discipline as an emanation of the logical requirements of their own minds and of their perception of the world instead of something essentially imposed from the outside which they have no choice but to accept unquestioningly.

All teachers present math to a considerable extent as a reflection of reality and will recognize in what I present constant reminders of what they already know and do. But all of us also, as we "teach math," find it easy to neglect that dimension of mathematics in the name of a mistaken quest for efficiency or just because that's how it has always been done.

So how do we teach the important number-sense concepts demonstrated by our shopper?

We do so in any number of ways, not significantly different for the most part from what teachers do routinely as they seek to teach addition and subtraction facts to first and second graders.

Our shoppers know that the total cost for the items and discount coupons in the cart is already determined, that it will not be changed as items are randomly pulled out of the cart and scanned. We can communicate that understanding by giving first graders a handful of cents that they count. They find 21. That's like the total value in the cart. We put those cents at random in three plates. Children who have reached a stage of mental development where it makes sense to teach them how to add remain convinced that they still have 21 cents. They prove the teacher wrong and feel empowered as the teacher, playacting, tries to convince them that the total changes as the plates are moved around or as two plates are combined into one.

We may also tease them into formulating their understanding: "Let's pretend I am going to give you all those coins. Do you want them when they are in two plates or in three? Who wants them when I have them in three plates? Who doesn't care? Why not?" They understand that if the total changed, it would be magic, not common sense. Our role is to identify and treasure that intuitive understanding, help students identify it themselves, formulate it, and anchor it in their psyche.

On these very simple topics, mathematical truths can be experienced and described in ways that, essentially, allow students to just take them for granted. Back home, asked what they have learned today, they can truthfully give the standard answer: "Nothin'."

Our shoppers understand that the order in which numbers are added does not affect the total. To communicate this to children, let's give them a small handful of quarters, dimes, and nickels (or tokens with appropriate numbers) and ask them to add them. They are encouraged to find adding strategies. It soon makes a lot of sense to pick 4 quarters and set them aside: that's a dollar. They can make another dollar with 3 quarters, 2 dimes, and a nickel. They may end up with three piles of a dollar each and 45 cents. With the coins initially spread out randomly in front of them, there is no order. If there is no order, clearly, the order doesn't matter. Children can be helped to experience, notice, and formulate that the flexibility in moving numbers around and in grouping them does not disappear when those numbers are finally aligned in some formal sequence of additions. They can still pick and choose as they add in any way they want. This claims for formal mathematics what comes naturally to our shoppers. It does so in a way that is natural and unthreatening. It just makes sense. But it doesn't apply when subtractions are included in the sequence.

To include subtractions, we need to go back to the central understanding of those shoppers.

> A $4.00 box of cereal adds $4.00 to my total bill. A $1.00 discount coupon reduces my total bill by $1.00.

Each number is unavoidably linked in the minds of those shoppers with a need to add or to subtract. It comes naturally to them as the numbers represent a price tag on an item purchased or a dollar amount on a discount coupon. So as the items or coupons are grouped or change position, they carry along with them the implication that each amount is either added or subtracted. This can be transferred to abstract sequences of additions and subtractions by helping students acquire a mental picture that operation signs + or − apply to the number that follows. The sign and number combination cannot be separated.

This perspective can be illustrated and communicated by using bubbles around a number and the operation sign in front of it. A shopper's experience at the checkout counter could be illustrated as follows:

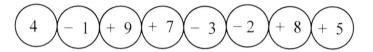

The bubbles can be moved around and grouped with as much freedom as the bottle of apple juice or discount coupon that they represent. Using or imagining these bubbles with an abstract sequence of additions and subtractions provides the same freedom and flexibility. That perspective comes naturally to teachers—but not always so for children who might otherwise be tempted to group $1 + 9$ or calculate $3 - 2$ in the sequence.

Once equipped with the understanding, children can use the freedom that it gives in strategies to add and subtract. They can learn to select pairings that are easy to add, such as "make-10" pairs. The Common Core State Standards recommend such strategies (see 1.OA.6). Students pull out 3 and 7 to one side, that's a 10; 14 and -4 form another pair with a value of 10. They are left with a single tile, for instance -1. They count: 10 ... 20 ... 19. Children can do this with formal sequences of numbers added and subtracted, crossing out combinations as they are identified:

$$14 - 1 + 3 - 4 + 7 = 19$$

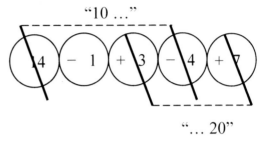

Such strategies for adding and subtracting communicate to our students that creativity pays. They empower students and give them a sense of ownership in addition and subtraction practices that could otherwise be routine and soporific. They confirm their understanding that mathematics is an activity of the mind.

These bubbles are going to be our secret weapon to communicate to students a number-sense understanding that comes quite naturally to our shoppers. They help children associate each operation sign with the number that follows. We don't just have 1; we have 1 that is subtracted. We don't just have 3; we have 3 that is added. The bubbles highlight that connection. They are a simple and practical pedagogical tool that helps us claim for formal mathematics our shoppers' intuitive understanding concerning the box of cereal and the discount coupon, an understanding that our students may or may not acquire on their own with numbers unattached to things.

The bubbles, we may point out, are not parentheses and will normally be presented to students long before they hear about multiplication or use parentheses to signify multiplication. Also, until negative numbers are introduced, the initial number must be an amount that is added, and the sign for addition reappears if it is moved to another position. This does not represent a difficulty.

Initially, some children may find it difficult to draw those bubbles around the appropriate sign and number combination. So we may ask them to first put a dot immediately behind each number and to draw these bubbles by going from one dot to the next and then back again. Doing so helps students focus on "− 2" instead of "2 +", which is precisely the understanding we want to communicate. The bubbles, of course, are used to communicate an understanding that remains after they are discarded.

What is the alternative often used to help students move numbers around and combine them in a sequence of additions and subtractions?

What we have just proposed may seem so obvious, so natural that some may ask, isn't that what is always done, one way or another? Unfortunately, it is not. In practice, the alternative approach to teach students how to move numbers around, vigorously recommended by the Common Core State Standards, is an appeal to the commutative and associative properties of operations. But we don't need the commutative property to teach students that $5 + 2 = 2 + 5$. All it takes is a 5-2 domino where students learn to see 7 dots whether it is shown as $5 + 2$ or turned around and read as $2 + 5$. Children don't need to learn that the commutative property does not apply to subtraction to know that $5 - 2$ is not equal to $2 - 5$. All they need, before they learn about negative numbers, is an intuitive understanding that you cannot take away more than you have. A conversation on the topic can be initiated by giving a student 2 tokens and asking her to give you 5 back. Teachers can devise any number of activities to confirm and claim for mathematics that $4 + 7 + 3 = 4 + 10$. Students can know these facts without having to pay tribute to the troll of the commutative and associative properties hiding under the bridge.

The commutative and associative properties describe characteristics of operations. They represent a vision that stands in contrast to the vision demonstrated by our shoppers and highlighted by the bubbles. They are not the best tool to process our ability to move numbers around and group them. The commutative property states that $5 + 2 = 2 + 5$ and points out that the operation sign stays unchanged in the middle while the two numbers switch position. This is a valid perception but not one that attaches the $+$ sign to the number that follows. Based on their understanding of what happens to their total cost as they pull an item from the shelf, the shoppers' equally valid perspective binds the signs for addition or subtraction to the number that follows. That alternative perspective gives full flexibility to move sign and number combinations around and group them creatively. It also applies to subtraction.

The approach suggested by the shoppers essentially replaces procedure with number sense and understanding. Requiring students to refer to those two properties of operations to move numbers around is essentially unteaching compared to the ease that could be theirs almost naturally or with a minimum of gentle prodding. There is a gap there between different ways of understanding what it means to know math that is not unrelated to more serious gaps in achievement and national standing. Children required to justify each move by referring to a property know less math, not more, than those with the more intuitive understanding.

Faced with a sequence of additions and subtractions, who knows more math: the child who understands that each operation sign applies to the number that follows and uses that understanding to change + 159 and − 59 found anywhere in the sequence into an even 100, or the child who finds himself powerless and at a loss because he has been trained to justify each move by the name of a property and remembers that those properties apply to addition, not subtraction?

Let's ask any teacher to evaluate mentally a sequence such as this one, perhaps pencil in hand to cross out numbers that have been processed:

$$96 - 59 + 4 + 159$$

I can imagine the teacher combining 96 and 4 to get 100 and then 159 and − 59 for a second 100 and the final value—all without any consideration given to the properties of operations. Sometimes, teaching to intuition is as simple as looking inward and asking ourselves how we process information and explain things to ourselves.

> We will return to these shoppers and to these bubbles later, when we look at the Common Core State Standards. We will then be in a better position to understand why our shoppers' intuitive ability to manipulate these numbers is so much more powerful and flexible than what is provided by the more traditional reliance on properties of operations.

So let's learn from these shoppers and the breadth of their intuitive understanding.

They demonstrate a trust in their intuitive perception that manifests itself not in the abstraction of paper and pencil mathematics but as it is applied to modeling and manipulating reality. The Common Core State Standards for Mathematical Practice are an urgent plea to use mathematics to model, understand, and shape the real world in which we live. They make it clear that the objective of using mathematics to model reality is a powerful transformative force in helping us rethink how we teach mathematical content. Our attempt to transfer to formal mathematics the intuitive understanding of our shoppers is an example of that transformative force in action.

In the perspective of allowing our mathematical knowledge to bear on the daily activities of our lives, can we imagine the same easy confidence in our shoppers, the same willingness to pay for the sandwiches and the chicken wings either at the deli or at the checkout counter, if the grouping they practiced needed to be processed in their minds by the associative property of addition?

The shoppers' understanding is shared by all, whether mathematically gifted or less so, fluent in English or less so. When claimed by formal mathematics, it does not depend as much on wording. There is equity in that kind of understanding. In fact, even native English-speaking students may experience as an extra hurdle the need to keep straight which is the commutative and which is the associative property.

Teaching to Intuition is based on the premise that we can anchor much of our students' essential mathematical knowledge to their common-sense understanding of preexisting mathematical realities and mental patterns. That quality in the knowledge, our students' sense of ownership in the material, can remain even as topics become significantly more sophisticated. The cumulative effect of doing so, on one topic after another, amounts to a profound change in what we understand as knowing math. It means more knowledge, not less; more understanding, more thinking, better habits of mind, a more reliable number sense, a greater ability to apply the knowledge to model the world we live in, and a greater propensity to enjoy and embrace the discipline. It may help reverse long-held convictions by some of our students that they are not good at math and never will be.

In the process, our aim is to open wide our students' ability and willingness to meet the challenges of a world modeled by technology, science, and innovation.

2

Operations on Fractions

Operations on fractions are a major cause of frustration for students and teachers. Along with operations on integers, the topic may be the most significant hurdle preventing students from moving on smoothly into algebra. The challenge remains through elementary and middle school and into high school. Many still need to take college remedial classes on the topic. Some students "get it," others don't, despite years of being given the same rules to remember and apply. And precisely, that's the problem. For each of the four operations, there may be a need to multiply the denominator of one of the fractions by the numerator or denominator of the other. Students then experience operations on fractions as a tangle of rules, mastered by some, forming for others one big, confusing procedural mess. Without understanding, it is difficult to sort it all out. Let's try *teaching to intuition* on this major topic.[*]

In the detailed modeling that follows, we attempt to bring back into the fold of intuition a sizable chunk of arithmetic on fractions, the more difficult part: adding and subtracting. Doing so should make it easier for

---

[*] A shorter version of this strategy was part of my article "Teaching to Intuition" in the National Council of Teachers of Mathematics' publication *Mathematics Teaching in the Middle School,* November 2011.

students not just to add and subtract fractions but to master what is left out here: multiplication and division.

To immediately focus on the essential, we are putting ourselves in a remedial setting. This allows us to assume some prior knowledge on the part of students, for instance of equivalent fractions.

Simplifying Fractions

For this strategy to apply, we must first make a consistent effort to separate operations on fractions from the need to simplify fractions. The reason is simple: a simplified answer hides the understanding. Purely as an illustration of the addition of whole numbers, it does not make much sense to say, "21 inches + 3 inches = 2 feet." The logic of addition just doesn't show. So we want to avoid the compulsive need on the part of some students to simplify fractions as a necessary step in finding the answer. We want to separate *in their minds* the process of adding and subtracting from the process of reducing to simplest terms or changing into mixed numbers. When given a correct but unsimplified answer, our attitude should be "Good. You have the right answer. Is there anything else you can do to make your answer even better?" The same objective may also affect how we grade operations on fractions, with correct but unsimplified answers receiving at least some recognition. Here, at the right time, we will tell our students that we absolutely do not want to simplify fractions. We will not change 8/8 into 1!

Three Important Questions

After years of frustration, students may be turned off when told that the class is going to review operations on fractions. So there is no need to mention fractions and announce our ultimate objective before we start a conversation. The *three important questions* we are going to ask are not necessarily linked to fractions. We just announce to the class that we are going to ask them three important questions. After a short buildup of the expectation, we ask the questions. The first two hit the students as anticlimactic: "What's so important about that?"

1st important question: What's 5 dogs + 3 dogs?

2nd important question: What's 5 cats + 3 cats?

3rd important question: What's 5 dogs + 3 cats?

In contrast, the third question leads to some initial confusion and a variety of answers. Most are correct, including "You can't add them!" I have yet to find a class where at least one student doesn't answer "8 animals!" or "8 pets!" Let's congratulate the class on the different answers and agree that 8 pets is one of the correct answers. Let's even agree to make it our common answer.

What's important with the three questions, of course, is not the questions themselves but the discussion and the discovery that they facilitate. The primary objective is to help students become aware of and formulate the thinking process *that has already occurred in their minds* as they answered these questions. Students catch on quickly. But we cannot be satisfied with just hints that students have understood. We will use whatever time it takes for notions to sink in and for students to formulate them clearly.

I am presenting here the teacher's side of an *imaginary dialogue* with a class. The teacher seeks to draw answers from the class and echoes to some extent some of those answers. Apart from that echoing, I am leaving to the reader's imagination the answers students may give. This is not a script to be followed, just a possible option.

The class has just answered the three important questions. The dialogue continues.

Teacher:

> Arithmetic told you, "5 + 3 = 8." Why didn't you answer, "8 dogs"?

> So logic told you, "I don't have 8 dogs. I don't have 8 cats. I can't add cats and dogs because they are different!" Is that right?

> Why didn't you answer "8 chairs" instead of "8 pets"?

> You thought, "Dogs are pets, and cats are pets. Let's add 5 pets and 3 pets." And you gave "8 pets" as

your answer to my question about cats and dogs. That's a lot of thinking.

Could you answer "8 pets" without thinking about all of this?

Did you know that you were thinking all of this? Perhaps not. Sometimes our thinking hides from us. Sometimes it even hides itself as hesitation or even confusion.

Here or elsewhere, we may want to expand on that important point.

Were any of you a little bit confused when I asked that third question about cats and dogs? Your brain thinks, "5 + 3 = 8. But I don't have 8 dogs. I don't have 8 cats. What am I supposed to do?" That's good thinking. But perhaps the only thing you are aware of is confusion. Some of you probably thought, "What does the teacher really want me to say?"

Mathematics is a thinking process, and confusion is part of that thinking process. If you accept that, if you welcome confusion or hesitation as a step in the thinking process, then you can move on from there. You need to listen to your brain—and confusion is your brain speaking loud and clear. You need to ask your brain some questions: "Hey, brain, why are you confused? What's bothering you? You know that 5 and 3 is 8, but you don't have 8 dogs or 8 cats. Is that what's bothering you? Let me help you out. You don't have 8 dogs, but you have 8 pets, don't you?"

Or we can immediately follow through on our discussion of the three important questions:

Let's make a diagram of what went on in your mind.

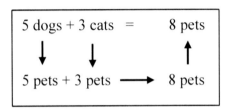

You change cats and dogs into pets.
Now you have the same name, and you can add.

Can you think of other examples where the same thing happens in your mind, where you need to change the name before you can add?

Your aunt has 3 daughters and 2 sons. Can you add them?

There are 10 boys and 15 girls in a classroom …
There are 10 boys and 15 girls on a bus …
There are 3 teachers and 2 parents in the yard …

Let me ask you, "What's 5 dogs and 3 songs?"
You seem to find that question difficult.
Can someone explain why it is almost impossible to add 5 dogs and 3 songs?

This kind of adding, where you change boys and girls into students or passengers, or cats and dogs into pets, you've done it all your life, haven't you? You and I just became a little bit more aware of what we already knew.

So we agree: you can only add things that have the same name. When you really want to add things that have a different name, you must first give them a common name.

Back to Fractions

Fractions are the topic of the day, but so far, we have not mentioned fractions. In fact, we could move in a different direction. We could, for instance, help students discover a connection between what they have just experienced with cats and dogs and what our shoppers also knew intuitively: that you can only add things that have the same name. We could seek other incarnations of that basic truth. But we are committed to reviewing operations on fractions. At this stage, without any need for a transition, we can do so. We write one on the board (e.g., 3/4). Let's continue with one side of an imaginary dialogue.

$\frac{3}{4}$ Three quarters. What do you call the top part?

What does "numerator" mean, do you think?

"Numerous." "Innumerable." "Enumerate." "Numerator." What idea do all these words have in common?

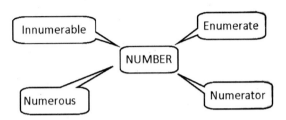

We can count: 1 quarter, 2 quarters, 3 quarters; 1 fifth, 2 fifths, 3 fifths. Why do you think the top number in a fraction is called the numerator? It means *number*, and it represents the number of parts, doesn't it?

What about denominator? What does that mean?

When you *nominate* someone student body president, is it the same thing as *naming* that person a candidate for president?

My neighbor sold his car to his son for a *nominal* price. That means very cheap. Perhaps for only a dollar! It's a price in *name* only, not in reality.

To nominate. Nominal. Denominator. They all mean *name*.

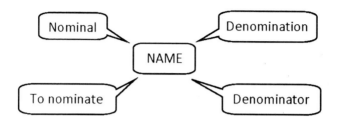

The denominator is the name of the part. When we write a fraction, both numerator and denominator are numbers. But when we read a fraction or spell it out, the numerator remains a number but the denominator is a name: a quarter, a third, a fifth, a tenth. It takes an *s* in the plural: 3 quarters, 2 thirds, 4 fifths.

So: $\frac{3}{4} = \frac{\text{NUMERATOR}}{\text{DENOMINATOR}} \quad = \quad \frac{\text{NUMBER (of parts)}}{\text{NAME (of the part)}}$

We can think of a fraction in many different ways. Right now, what will help us most is to think of 3 quarters as 3 of something called a quarter and of 2 ninths as 2 of something called a ninth.

In the same way:

> 2 fifths is 2 of something called a fifth.
> 4 elevenths is …
> 9 tenths is …

Teachers know too much. It is easy for them to think in terms of their better students and to conclude that their explanations are validated when those better students show that they understand. Here, the weaker students in the class may take part in echoing, "9 tenths is 9 of something called a tenth," without fully assuming the understanding of a fraction as a given number of equal parts. To help them, I may have them count those separate parts with me as an introduction to the questions that follow:

"Let's count each part:
1 quarter, 2 quarters,
3 quarters, 4 quarters."

"1 eighth, 2 eighths,
3 eighths, ... 8 eighths."

What's 3 eighths plus 3 eighths?

What's 2 ninths plus 5 ninths?
   (You're not sure? What's 2 books plus 5 books?)
What's 3 sixteenths plus 2 sixteenths?
What's 3 eighths of an inch plus 4 eighths of an inch?
What's 3 fifths minus 1 fifth?
What's 2 ninths multiplied by 4?
   (What's 2 dollars multiplied by 4?)
What's 15 sixteenths divided by 3?
What's 7 tenths plus 2 tenths?

It seems that you know quite a lot about adding, subtracting, multiplying, and dividing fractions. Sometimes it's no different from adding books or students:

4 books + 2 books = 6 books.
So: 4 tenths + 2 tenths = 6 tenths.

4 students × 3 = 12 students.
So: 4 sixteenths × 3 = 12 sixteenths.

I call *lazymath* any strategy where common sense understanding allows us to perform elementary mathematics—on this and other topics—without applying the usual set of rules, or even any rule at all. The word draws students' attention to what is taking place. When students use a procedural approach when a common-sense shortcut is available, we may ask them, "Could you also use lazymath?" Here, we are using lazymath on arithmetic with fractions. I constantly meet students so overwhelmed by rules that they have completely lost touch with the possibility of that lazymath approach to operations on fractions. Rediscovering it is a revelation that contrasts and chips away at their perception of operations on fractions as some monstrous mathematical aberration that they will never master.

The approach, of course, has its limitations. We can only ask questions where fractions can be added, subtracted, multiplied, or divided without changing the denominator. So at that stage, we do the following:

- We only ask students to add and subtract fractions that have or have already been given a common denominator. After all, these are the only fractions that can be added.
- We only ask them to divide when the numerator is divisible by the divisor.
- We don't allow them to simplify, even when it would be obvious and easy to do so.

We allow the class to practice lazymath arithmetic on fractions long enough for it to become obvious and automatic. We want students to experience some kind of shock when they are finally confronted with having to add fractions that have different denominators. We want them not just to know but to experience *the need for a common denominator* in the same way as they discovered the need to change cats and dogs into pets. Let's continue with our imaginary dialogue. We are ready for the kill.

I am going to ask you three questions. Listen to your brain as you answer.

What's 5 eighths plus 2 eighths?
What's 5 ninths plus 2 ninths?
What's 5 eighths plus 2 ninths?

Did you find it easy to add 5 eighths and 2 eights?
But you're not sure about 5 eighths and 2 ninths, are you?

Do you remember hesitating like that fifteen minutes ago when I asked you three other questions? What were those questions? Can someone explain?

Do you mean it's like cats and dogs? You can only add fractions that have the same denominator? What did we say *denominator* means?

We can only add things that have the same name. If things have different names, we must first give them a common name before we can add.

Give me two fractions that have the same denominator. Now add them.

Give me two fractions that have a different denominator. Are they as easy to add? What are you going to do if you really want to add those two fractions?

That's like changing cats and dogs into pets, isn't it?

Let's try to add 2/5 and 3/4. Can you change them both into pets?

The notion of equivalent fractions is a prerequisite to what we are doing here. Teachers will not present operations on fractions unless students have already become familiar with the separate topic of equivalent fractions. So we assume here that students find it easy to change $\underline{2}$ and $\underline{3}$ into $\underline{8}$ and $\underline{15}$. And we do so.
   5   4   20   20

Now that we have a common denominator, our students know how to add the fractions. We summarize what took place as follows, adding the box on the right to the diagram about cats and dogs.

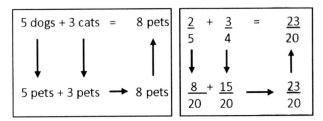

And the dialogue continues.

> Does this pattern seem familiar?
> This is exactly what we did when we tried to add dogs and cats, isn't it?
> Let's compare the two patterns.

We help students experience and understand that the procedures of mathematics for adding fractions reflect the thought pattern that was theirs when they tried to add dogs and cats and had to find a common name. They are shaped by the same fundamental logic that existed in their minds before any mathematical concerns.

> Does anybody want to explain to the class (can you discuss with your group) why we need to have a common denominator to add or subtract fractions?

A dialogue of this nature—it can be implemented in very different ways—throws a floodlight of intuition in the midst of the frustrating topic of operations on fractions.

- We connect with intuition when students experience using with fractions the familiar skills they use to add, subtract, multiply, or divide books or dollars. Lazymath brings home the point that "operations on fractions" is not a set of mathematical rules. It is tied to reality. Throughout the grades, we will never let students forget the lazymath option to operations on fractions.

- We connect with intuition when students *experience* the need for a common denominator as no different from the necessity of changing brothers and sisters into siblings or dogs and cats into pets when we want to add them. Students are not just given a rule. They are not just briefly reminded that you can't add apples and oranges as an explanation for that rule. The order is changed. The understanding comes *before* its application to mathematics. The students are guided to apply an intuitive rule of logic to cats and dogs, a setting where they do so naturally; they are helped to discover and formulate what they have just done. Only then are they given the opportunity to transfer the understanding to adding fractions.

It may not take more than a single class period to develop that connection with what our students have always known, but we aim to make it from then on the constant source of their knowledge about adding fractions. At every opportunity, in the months and years that follow, grade after grade, instead of being reminded of a rule, they will be reconnected with the experience.

After the understanding has been rekindled in their minds, it may then cautiously be summarized in the form of a rule about common denominators provided that this is seen as a description of what they already know or a backup formulation and not allowed to become the main source of their knowledge.

We take it for granted that students need repeated practice—they do, but we often assume that explanations can be given once. Reconnecting students with the understanding and the experience should remain the preferred option when students need to refresh their knowledge of the topic. It can be as simple as asking "What's 5 dollars and 3 dollars?" to a student tempted to add both numerators and denominators or asking, "What's 5 dogs and 3 cats?" to a student who needs a little push in the right direction.

> We are encountering here the essence of what it means to teach to intuition. Who knows more math: students who remember the rules and add them to their long collection of rules on this and other topics or students who add 3/7 and 2/7 as naturally as they would 3 books and 2 books, and who sense and perhaps even resent the impossibility of adding 3/7 and 2/9, and experience the need for substituting equivalent fractions with a common denominator?

Our three important questions are the key to the whole strategy. Students wallowing in rules and confusion suddenly realize they don't have to anymore. They say, "Wow! It makes sense!" The process speaks to their intuition. The rules are experienced by them as something that their own inner requirements impose on mathematics, not as something imposed on them by some outside authority. They are pursuing their quest for mathematical knowledge as something that they own, something that deserves their willing acquiescence. They feel empowered, and it shows in their eyes. At some point, they may connect their understanding about adding fractions with the understanding shared by shoppers at the checkout counter: you can only add things that have the same name. Understanding begins to build a network of connections in their minds.

3

Adding Integers

The temperature is 10° below zero, −10° Fahrenheit. At sunset, it goes down another 5°. There are millions of people with very little mathematical skills that correctly conclude that the temperature is now −15°. It makes sense because we know that −15° is 5° colder than −10°. I have a $100.00 overdraft in my checking account that shows up as −100.00 on my statement. I need to deposit funds to avoid a penalty. I make a $120.00 deposit. Like millions of people, many with very little mathematical skills, I conclude that I now have a $20.00 positive balance in my account. It makes sense because I am depositing $20.00 more than I need to. And yet, addition and subtraction that include negative numbers is a major hurdle for many of our students. It is initially taught in the last years of elementary school and, like operations on fractions, remains for too many a dreaded topic all the way to remedial classes in college.

Adding and subtracting integers is as pervasive and crucial in algebra as adding and subtracting counting numbers is to basic arithmetic. So over the grades and into college, students' inability to do so makes it almost impossible for them to seriously progress in algebra. Of course, many students master the topic, but the effect on those who don't is a confirmation of their fears, their dislikes, their insecurities, or just plainly their rejection of things mathematical. The cost for students, teachers, and taxpayers in time, money, and self-esteem is huge. The whole premise of *Teaching to Intuition* is to accept the fact that far too many students are left behind and that reversing that situation is not going to be achieved by doing what worked well for some students just a little bit better.

So on this particular topic, let's ask ourselves what it is that these millions intuitively know when faced with concrete situations and that so many students find so difficult once the numbers are considered in the abstract, unattached to actual things and devoid of any connection to actual situations.

Somewhat facetiously, let me say that it could well be what these millions don't know—or don't pay attention to—that gives them such an advantage. With a negative number, the larger its absolute value, the smaller the number: −15 is smaller, colder, lower below sea level, and more in debt than −10. When we subtract 5 from −10, the absolute value becomes larger. As a consequence, with the introduction of negative numbers, students are asked to break with a major assumption. In *regular* arithmetic (I will use this expression to refer to arithmetic before negative numbers), there is a complete identity between *operation* and *calculation*. We see an addition, and we add. We see a subtraction, and the calculation that we perform in our head, on paper, or with a calculator is a subtraction. Adding means adding, and subtracting means subtracting. How could it be any different? But with integers, this absolute identity between operation and calculation no longer applies.

The temperature is −10° and goes down another 5°. It is now −15°.

Here lies the central conundrum: the operation is a subtraction, but the calculation that gives the answer is an addition. The difficulty for many of our students is not so much learning the new as forgetting the old, a significantly more difficult task. It's like Simon Says: with negative numbers, students often need to resist the urge to subtract when they see a subtraction or add when they see an addition. Their minds formulate the dilemma as confusion.

There are different approaches to overcoming this apparent contradiction. One California-approved middle school textbook presents a solution as follows:

- To add integers with the same sign, add their absolute values. Give the result the common sign.
- To add integers with different signs, find the difference between the absolute values. Give the result the sign of the number with the greater absolute value.
- To subtract an integer, add its additive inverse.
  $$9 − 7 = 9 + (−7), \text{ or } 2$$

The approach gives three rules: the first two tell us how to add integers; the third tells us how to change a subtraction into an addition, which then allows us to apply one of the first two rules.

Let's see how it works using the very example given by the textbook, finding the value of $9 - 7$. The third rule tells us to change $9 - 7$ into $9 + (-7)$, which leads us to apply the second rule. It tells us to take the difference between the absolute values, in other words to calculate $9 - 7$. That should be easy, as that's exactly what the third rule tells us how to do, which sends us back to $9 + (-7)$. Do we have a vicious circle here? The set of rules works because students are wise enough to know when not to apply it. Wisdom tells them, "Just pretend that absolute values are not like other numbers, and get on with the job!"

Needless to say, for many students, the procedure works and guides students around the conundrum. Some students even make sense of it. But many don't. There are other approaches: with a number line, with tokens of a different color for positive and negative that are added or that cancel each other out. But essentially, these are only useful manipulatives.

When applied to practical situations, common sense reference points allow us to intuitively perceive that $-15°$ is $5°$ colder than $10°$ below zero. When dealing with numbers in the abstract, those points of references do not exist. The challenge for us teachers is to devise an approach that applies to mathematical expressions unattached to temperatures, money, altitudes, or colored tokens, and that still retains the power of evidence found in practical examples and in addition and subtraction of positive numbers. Such an approach implies a few changes to long-held traditions—not dramatic changes but real changes nevertheless.

These pages cannot become a detailed textbook. With the understanding that teachers will supplement as needed, let me highlight three of the teaching strategies that, working together, go a long way to meeting the challenge of making addition and subtraction of integers as intuitive as is its implementation in concrete situations.

Priority Given to One-Sign Formulations

The textbook we quoted instructed students to change 9 − 7 into 9 + (−7). This has the advantage of eliminating subtraction as an operation (while still retaining it as a calculation performed on absolute values). It also establishes two sets of rules: those that were used in regular arithmetic (before negative numbers) and a different set tailored to accommodate negative numbers. That is neither needed nor justified. We should try to expand the rules that apply to counting numbers so as to include negative numbers instead of replacing familiar rules in order to do so.

Instead of changing 9 − 7 into 9 + (−7), we choose to do the opposite. We allow students to become very familiar with one-sign formulations such as 9 − 7 or −10 − 5 before introducing their two-sign equivalent (9 + ⁻7 or −10 + ⁻5). When ultimately faced with two-sign formulations, we show students how to immediately change them back into the one-sign equivalent which they have learned to evaluate.

A Vertical Number Line

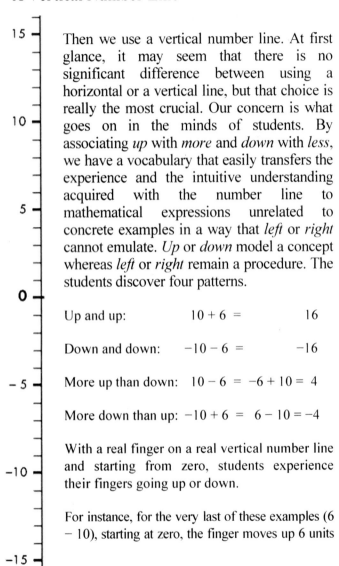

Then we use a vertical number line. At first glance, it may seem that there is no significant difference between using a horizontal or a vertical line, but that choice is really the most crucial. Our concern is what goes on in the minds of students. By associating *up* with *more* and *down* with *less*, we have a vocabulary that easily transfers the experience and the intuitive understanding acquired with the number line to mathematical expressions unrelated to concrete examples in a way that *left* or *right* cannot emulate. *Up* or *down* model a concept whereas *left* or *right* remain a procedure. The students discover four patterns.

Up and up: $10 + 6 = 16$

Down and down: $-10 - 6 = -16$

More up than down: $10 - 6 = -6 + 10 = 4$

More down than up: $-10 + 6 = 6 - 10 = -4$

With a real finger on a real vertical number line and starting from zero, students experience their fingers going up or down.

For instance, for the very last of these examples ($6 - 10$), starting at zero, the finger moves up 6 units

40

as $6.00 are earned and down 10 units as $10.00 are spent.

On the number line, with 6 − 10, the contrast between the up and down motions is experienced as one number canceling out in part the distance implied by the other number. It is experienced as a difference between the distances and described in terms that imply taking a difference between upward and downward motions. With 6 − 10, calculating a difference makes sense, as does the negative outcome.

The use of an actual number line is, of course, just an initial strategy used to experience an understanding. It can never accommodate the wide range of numbers that we encounter. As they learn to move away from an actual line, students can learn to use any point on page or table as the real zero of an imaginary vertical number line, from which a finger can move "down and down," "more down than up", and so on.

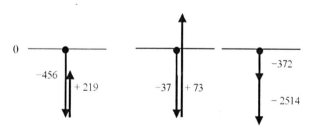

This can help students sort out whether distances are added or subtracted and whether the ending point is in positive or negative territory. That imaginary line remains available under any circumstances, including when the pressure of a test might otherwise add its own disruption to a more direct processing.

Bubbles

As a third strategy, initially, I like to put each number and the sign in front of it inside a bubble. The bubbles help focus a student's attention on what matters and away from what does not. They put in sharp contrast the two decisions that have to be made: a choice between a positive or negative value for the final answer and a choice between adding or subtracting as the calculation that gives us the magnitude.

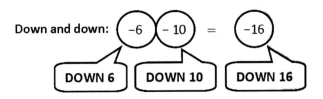

To put themselves in the place of their students, let's ask the readers to forget about absolute value, forget about subtraction, forget about additive inverse, forget about any equivalence between subtracting a positive and adding a negative, ignore the real difference between the two bubbles. Having banished all this from their thoughts, readers are asked to focus only on the similar message that each bubble gives about magnitude and direction: "down 6" and "down 10."

The pattern is "down and down." It is experienced with a finger on a vertical number line. Students feel their fingers pushed in the same downward direction by each bubble; they see the distances being added. They experience their fingers stopping well into negative territory, and they understand why. Pushing the finger in the same direction implies adding the distances. The downward motion confirms a negative answer. Seen in contrast to "up and up," a −16 value comes as naturally and intuitively as the positive 16 value of 6 + 10.

The perception acquired with the help of these bubbles remains after the bubbles are discarded. The valuation is achieved without any need to be processed by the mind in terms of rules, words, or procedures.

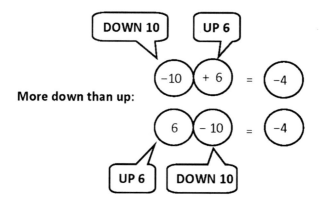

With or without the + sign, one bubble indicates an upward motion of the finger. Whether the minus sign is for a negative number or for subtraction, the other bubble implies a downward motion. The information inside the bubbles pushes the finger in opposite directions. The motions cancel each other out in part; they fight. "More down than up" and "more up than down" imply a subtraction. The "more" confirms a negative or positive value without any need to formulate the process in terms of "taking the difference between absolute values and giving the answer the sign of the number with the larger absolute value," even when that is indeed what is done.

Each bubble implies a magnitude and a direction. This is all that the finger needs to know as it moves on the number line. First with the bubbles and soon after without them, the valuation reflects a conceptual understanding of what each number represents as it is linked with the sign in front of it.

Given 10 and 6, both positive and negative, and the two operations of addition and subtraction, there are only four possible values: 16, −16, 4, −4. Students are helped to notice that there is no other option. This limits the choices the mind has to make: "Should I add or subtract the distances? Do I have a positive or a negative outcome?"

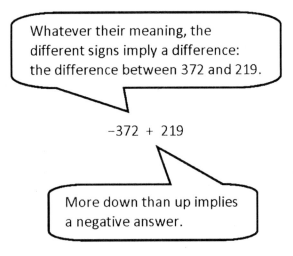

Whatever their meaning, the different signs imply a difference: the difference between 372 and 219.

−372 + 219

More down than up implies a negative answer.

> This is perceived without any need to be processed by the brain in terms of absolute values added or subtracted and then compared even when this is what is being done. The valuation could be described in those terms, but knowledge does not rely on the description.

After some practice, the correct conclusion can be reached at first glance, as intuitively as if these were temperature changes, with no concern for adding when the sign for the operation is a subtraction or subtracting when the sign is an addition. Thanks to the intuitive vocabulary made possible by the vertical number line, the mental processing acquired with number lines and bubbles remains even after bubbles and number lines are discarded.

When we finally expand to include two-sign formulations such as $10 + {}^-3$, students learn to cross out or disregard unneeded + signs and to associate a single – sign, whatever its meaning, as pushing the finger down. Students also need to be taught that two minus signs, as in $10 - {}^-3$, cancel out and are the equivalent of a single + sign. It is easy to find illustrations to confirm that, in mathematics as in real life, taking away a negative is a plus. On the number line, the first – sign is an invitation to move the finger down. Before that can be achieved, the second – sign cannot be ignored and is interpreted as inviting the finger to change direction and push the finger up. Knowledge tied to a verbal description in terms of "two negatives" is prone to misinterpretations. Here again, we seek to avoid entrusting the knowledge to a mere description and memorized words.

- So we choose to perform calculations first on *one-sign formulations*. This allows the familiar arithmetic learned with counting numbers to remain unchanged even as the patterns are expanded to include negative numbers.
- Then by using or imagining a *vertical number line*, we associate +, *up*, and *more* and −, *down*, and *less* in a way that blends experience, concept, and vocabulary and gives intuition its best chance to take hold.
- Finally, the *bubbles*, as an early assist, help students focus on the direction (up or down) implied by each number and away from the operation which is often misleading.

What Students Think

Introduced to this strategy, students familiar with other approaches comment, "I didn't know it was so simple." A teacher who tried the approach e-mailed me, "I have never actually been thanked after a lesson, but today I was. Many times." I demonstrated the approach to a fellow teacher, Mark, in an after-school remedial session he was teaching to failing eighth-grade students drawn from different middle school classes and to a few students sent down from a neighboring high school. The real feedback came months later. I didn't really know if I had convinced Mark, but he tried the approach the next semester with the seventy students in his two weaker eighth-grade Algebra Readiness classes. He had these comments:

I was very encouraged with some recent test results in my Algebra Readiness class. The weeks you spent teaching in the after-school intervention with me were invaluable. I compared test results with my colleague who taught a similar group of students with traditional methods. My classes (approximately seventy students) posted an 83 percent average on the test, almost 20 percent higher than the other classes. This was the highest test average all year for my students. This was extraordinary! Your insight into teaching children using intuition and knowledge that is already a part of their thinking is exciting to use.

Mark did not use the textbook for this topic but gave his students the regular chapter test.

It was a challenge to teach with the current curriculum. Everything was presented with a horizontal number line, and the students wanted to do what the book was doing. So for this chapter, I did not allow the students to use the book. When it came time to take the test, many of the questions asked them to interpret a horizontal number line. The students had no problem turning the paper sideways so that everything made sense. This also worked great for teaching opposites and absolute value.

Two things pleased me most on receiving the e-mail. First, that I had not taught the class myself: the grades were not the result of some particular gift that I might possess as a teacher. A colleague had borrowed an approach and some of the strategies and had integrated them into his own style of teaching. Others could too.

Then, Mark also commented on the students' reactions.

> There was an excitement in the class as they finally got it! They kept asking for more problems and were very engaged. I had so many students with lightbulbs turning on for the first time!

The seventy or so in Mark's Algebra Readiness classes were students who did not find math easy. Hence the middle-sixty grade that Mark was expecting from prior years' experience. And yet, *they were asking for more. They were engaged.*

> We all aim to promote in our students those "aha" moments that Mark's students experienced, some for the first time. They do not occur when a rule is remembered or even reluctantly understood. They are a testimony that a more intimate connection has been established with the facts of math, that the truths of math have found an echo deep within the psyche. As I see it, they occur when intuition has given its seal of approval to those truths. *Teaching to Intuition* presents an approach to learning math essentially through a variety of examples and strategies that teachers initially may like or dislike, approve of or dismiss. Students, more often than not, experience a change in their understanding of what it means to know math. In this particular case, a justifiably skeptical teacher was convinced by his students.

And what about those students I had taught in that after-school intervention class? I had dropped in as the class was already in progress, and I participated for an official total of three hours spread three times a week over three weeks. There had been no before and after test. But one of these students, by then in high school, came back to see Mark, his eighth-grade teacher, to tell him that he was getting Bs in his high school algebra class. He took pride and credit for his newfound success, but he also referred to what he had learned in that after-school intervention class from that guy who dropped in on them, saying it was something he used every day.

> I imagine the frustrating encounter with algebra throughout their high school years for students who have not mastered arithmetic on positive and negative numbers. I think of those remedial classes in community colleges where operations on integers remains a major topic. I look at statistics on students who do not successfully pass algebra classes in high school. I imagine the cost: time, money, self-esteem. It doesn't have to be so. In very concrete ways, on this and other topics, strategies can be found that alleviate the difficulties and move students forward. This is the kind of change that *Teaching to Intuition* wants to accomplish.

Step by Step

Is this the best we can do? I hope that no one ever reaches that conclusion for any strategy or pedagogical approach, including those I may devise and propose to colleagues. We need to constantly keep our ears to the ground for difficulties that our students may have. In Mark's e-mail, it is clear that the students found it difficult to switch from the familiar horizontal number line to the vertical version. It is also clear that Mark had no choice but to present the material as a single unit, with all the material on the menu when the chapter on operations on integers came up in the textbook. So let me dream that those two impediments can be lifted.

Let me dream that his students are already familiar with a vertical number line and have used one as their standard version since first grade. Let's also imagine that Mark's students are allowed to explore the new freedom provided by negative numbers gradually, one new pattern at a time. "I have great news for you! Now that we have negative numbers, we can take away more than we have! You are familiar with $10 - 6 = 4$. Now we also have $6 - 10 = -4$. You can take away more than you have!" Students are allowed to become perfectly comfortable with the contrast. They model the math with practical situations. They understand that the difference remains the same even as it can be either positive or negative. They experience it with a finger on a vertical line. They describe the contrast in terms of "more up than down" or "more down than up." They use bubbles to learn to switch numbers around and learn to read $-6 + 10$ as the familiar $10 - 6$.

When that has become familiar, they explore another pattern. "Now that we have negative numbers, we can start with a negative number and keep going down from there." So students learn in similar ways to contrast $10 + 6 = 16$ and $-10 - 6 = -16$. They become very familiar with that new pattern. Students gradually explore all the patterns and become familiar with each one.

On this crucial topic, a class average of 83 percent is not good enough.

Absolute Value

In teaching addition and subtraction of integers as above, we use a finger on a vertical number line and use only words that the finger itself can understand: up, down, distances, and their relative magnitude. Though we may transgress on occasion, we feel no urge initially to speak of *absolute value* and certainly no inclination to require students to use the expression or depend on it to understand the new material. New words can be threatening. Their meaning, however simple, can take some time to sink in. If we define absolute value in terms of distance, we can for quite some time use *distance* instead of *absolute value*. We are not offending the gods of mathematics if, as we refer to adding 10 and 6 in $-10 - 6$, we speak of adding "two numbers." The absolute value of a number is a number. We want the truth, but not necessarily the whole truth just quite yet.

Are we shortchanging mathematics as we do so? I don't think so. In fact, once the calculations are mastered, I will have a long conversation with my class on the topic of absolute value.

Key ideas are the *arbitrary* and *relative* nature of negative numbers, their use as a *convenience* more than a reality. My students will understand that, however we choose to use positive and negative numbers to manipulate money earned and money owed, only real dollars change hands when the transaction is finally settled. They will reach the conclusion that, if I use negative numbers to sort out financial transactions, which side I choose as I illustrate who owes money to whom is arbitrary. A change of perspective could change the sign on all the balances. They will come to the conclusion that, if negative altitudes are convenient when mapping Death Valley in contrast to neighboring Mount Whitney, scuba divers have no need for negative numbers when measuring their depth below sea level, as they have no need to contrast their distance below the surface to distances above sea level.

We will also talk about temperature scales and contrast degrees Fahrenheit and degrees Celsius. We will highlight the arbitrary nature of these units by noticing that some temperatures are negative in one scale and positive in the other. We will discuss the nature of heat, how it is a measure of the motion of atoms and molecules. We may have students experience a frozen solid state by having a group of them lock arms and make it difficult for anyone to go through; a liquid state when, needing to shake their arms and turn around, they just stand near each other, making it easy for someone to push his way through; and the state where wild motions of arms and legs force everyone to move as far away from others as possible, mimicking the state of a gas and water vapor. Why learn math if it is not used as a window opening up on science?

If heat is motion, we will discuss what happens as the motion of atoms decreases, how a temperature exists where the thermal motion of atoms and molecules stops. We will ask students, "When there is no motion left, can it get any colder?" They will learn (or perhaps one will suggest) that this is what happens at −459° Fahrenheit, or absolute zero, a zero that is no longer *relative* or *arbitrary*. Absolute zero is used as zero in the Kelvin scale, a temperature scale that does not need and has no way of accommodating negative temperatures. In the end, those students will establish a connection between absolute zero and absolute value, seeing in both a reality not affected by arbitrary and relative perspectives. They will retain a much richer understanding of absolute value than if it had been presented essentially as a mathematical definition.

The Number Line

11

10

9

8

7

6

5

4

3

2

1

0

Let's ask ourselves, "Which is more intuitive: a horizontal number line or a vertical one? Which better corresponds to our experience of thermometers, altitudes, and most graphs? Which more intuitively reflects the very notions of 'more' and 'less'?" The answer seems obvious. And yet, most often, the horizontal version stretches around classroom walls. We even speak of "higher" and "lower" numbers as our fingers move right and left on a horizontal number line! We are so accustomed that we may not appreciate how changing to a vertical line might affect a child's ability to connect with essential number-sense perceptions that we are otherwise seeking to teach. We have just used a vertical number line as an important component in our strategy to teach addition and subtraction of integers. Its use is just as important in earlier grades.

We use a number line for a purpose. That purpose cannot be a mechanical tool for adding or subtracting. Students use their fingers on the number line to add and subtract in the early grades only as a means of building understanding. Students soon graduate to numbers too large and diverse to fit on a number line. Its purpose is to create an image in the mind, an image that students can use to better visualize addition and subtraction problems and the relative value of various numbers long after any actual number line has been discarded. The benefits of a number line are in its presence not on classroom walls but in the minds of our students. So why not imprint in their minds, right from the start, the more intuitive vertical version?

A small change such as this one wouldn't matter if all our students moved happily along the increasing sophistication of our curriculum as they go from grade to grade. But that is not so. Significant percentages are left behind. The answer cannot be in just doing what we have always done just a little bit better. The answer means change. Nobody claims that changing to a vertical number line is the answer. But if it has any chance of making things easier, why not use one?

Teaching to intuition is not an abstraction. The math remains essentially the same though some priorities might be rearranged. It's how mathematical truths are perceived by our students that changes; it's what we understand as knowing math—and therefore teaching math—that is readjusted. For us, implementation is carried out in very concrete steps, steps that it may be easy to dismiss but also easy to implement.

I see these small steps as having a cumulative effect far beyond their immediate benefit. A vertical number line may help first graders as they add and subtract, but it also makes it easier for sixth and seventh graders by then long familiar with it to apply it to integers. It strengthens number sense. Intractable problems begin to fade away. Teaching to intuition, if we want it to be more than a few strategies on this or that topic, implies opening our imaginations to trivial details and looking at long-held customs with a new sensitivity. In my mind, the routine use of a vertical number line can be one of those small steps with significant consequences.

The Itsy-Bitsy Spider

I have never taught first grade, but I had the opportunity of volunteering daily over three months in a first-grade class. I was soon given my own twenty-five-minute period, and every time, during the first five or so minutes, we would feed the spider.

I wanted the children to experience a vertical number line and thought of the itsy-bitsy spider and its waterspout as something they could better relate to than a number line. A discarded wooden slat from a window shade served as the number line. It had large numbers and a line made of Velcro. The spider also, with its plastic legs squeezed between two Lego pieces, had a Velcro belly. Our spider specialized in moving from single-digit to two-digit numbers or vice versa. It would always stop at 10 on its way up or down. That's where it got its snack.

A few children each day would come up to the spider at the front of the class, one at a time. They were given different instructions on what the spider wanted to do that morning. They would work out the instruction with the spider and the waterspout and then face the class and tell fellow students what had taken place: "The spider was on 7. It wanted to go up 5 steps. It took 3 steps to 10 and 2 more steps to 12." "The spider was on 14. It wanted to go down to 8. It took 4 steps to 10 and 2 more steps down to 8, for a total of 6 steps." I could adjust the challenge to the student's ability—or to the child's height. I could help if needed as the student acted out the instructions with spider in hand. Of course, the instructions given were somewhat coordinated with what the students were learning in other ways, from me and from the regular teacher. I remain stunned by how much they loved that spider. I once received a note from the teacher that read, "Jessica has not been called up yet this week. She is crying." One very weak student was normally given special instruction on the side on most topics and activities. He volunteered to be called up to feed the spider, and for some reason, as he correctly described what his spider had done, his fellow students applauded.

In the process, the children were becoming acquainted with a vertical number line. They were practicing breaking up numbers into components (5 into 3 and 2, for instance, as the spider took 3 steps to reach 10 and 2 more steps to achieve its goal of moving 5 steps up or down). They were learning to use a benchmark as a tool in thinking out addition and subtraction situations. They were acquiring knowledge, tools, and practice in the habit of using mental math. The hope was that the experience would expand during their years of schooling and become a lifelong habit as they naturally, casually, daily model through the lens of mathematics the world we live in and the information we receive. Mathematics is not the only perspective through which we should appraise our environment as consumers, citizens, and active participants, but in this age of information, science, and technology, it should be an important component.

Basic addition and subtraction math facts were grouped and practiced in different categories: doubling; adding 1 understood as counting; adding 2 understood as counting with even or with odd numbers; and so on. In contrast to earlier standards that essentially required students to commit to memory for immediate recall, these are strategies recommended by the Common Core State Standards (see Content Standards, Grade 1, Operations and Algebraic Thinking, No. 6):

> Use strategies such as counting on; making ten (e.g., $8 + 6 = 8 + 2 + 4 = 10 + 4 = 14$); decomposing a number leading to a ten (e.g., $13 - 4 = 13 - 3 - 1 = 10 - 1 = 9$); using the relationship between addition and subtraction (e.g., knowing that $8 + 4 = 12$, one knows $12 - 8 = 4$); and creating equivalent but easier or known sums (e.g., adding $6 + 7$ by creating the known equivalent $6 + 6 + 1 = 12 + 1 = 13$).

The children were becoming familiar with the all-important "make 10" facts that show how far a single-digit number is from 10. They practiced that with the spider and also in other ways. For instance, they played Go Fish with the required pairs made up, not of two 7s as usual, but of a "make 10" pair, a 7 and a 3 or a 2 and an 8.

The children experienced many incarnations of the important "5+" facts (5 + 3, 5 + 1, 5 + 4) including tally bars, nickel and cents, dominoes, actual numbers, and roman numerals. The children learned to see 7 when shown all the fingers of one hand and two fingers of another hand. They saw the connection with "make 10" facts when asked how many fingers were hidden.

The "5+" facts would later help children learn to double single-digit numbers. Children's ability to see 7 as 5 + 2 can be exploited as a strategy for knowing how to double 7. A child who learns to read roman numeral VII as 7 can be helped to see the 4 of 14 in VII + VII. I did not forget that a high school senior put me on the path to thinking seriously about how to teach math facts when, as he needed to divide 14 by 2 to simplify the fractional answer to an algebra problem, he suggested 6. My facial reaction prompted him to make a second offer: 8. I'm a nice guy, and we compromised, settling on the average of his two suggestions. After all, this was a math class.

The notions of even and odd played a part in some of the strategies: students perceived the odd man out in odd numbers; they experienced and explained that two even numbers have a sum that is even (where would the odd man out come from?) and that two odd numbers also have an even sum (the two odd men out finally find a teammate).

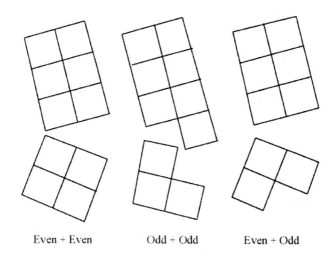

Even + Even   Odd + Odd   Even + Odd

We want children and the adults they become to know essential math facts. That knowledge is the key to simple, routine mental math that can become second nature, a habit of mind practiced as we attempt to make sense of information or compare purchases. Much of the routine practice where mathematics is used to enlighten for us the world in which we live is not done with pen and paper or with a calculator but on the spur of the moment, in our minds. Knowing basic math facts is an essential requirement if math is to be a living component of our daily lives.

Learning those facts is essential and deserves careful planning and strategies on the part of teachers. Giving equal emphasis to all the possible combinations and dumping them all on children as they are introduced or practiced is no strategy at all. It leads to endless drilling on the full range of essential facts in a hopeless endeavor to achieve automatic recall. It will work with some students but will never work for others.

The alternative is to follow the approach suggested by the Common Core Standards: selecting fewer facts for automatic recall and, for the others, developing mental strategies that create "equivalent but easier or known sums."

So the vertical number line was not the only tool. It was part of an array of strategies helping students learn addition and subtraction facts. But beyond the facts, it communicated a powerful number-sense understanding of addition and subtraction. Later, we can imagine adults who, faced with a need to evaluate $37 - 24$ for instance, as one option might think of moving up from 24 to 30, a 6-step journey, and then 7 more steps to 37, for a difference of 13. Thus, $37 - 24$ is replaced with the easier calculation $6 + 7$—all in the footsteps of the itsy-bitsy spider.

In Perspective

Let's take a step back to put the vertical number line and what we are trying to do here in perspective.

When I first arrived in Los Angeles in the early '70s there were frequent episodes of very severe air pollution. Los Angeles is in a basin, surrounded by mountains, and under some weather conditions, what happens in Los Angeles stays in Los Angeles. The fumes that we create linger and accumulate for days instead of blowing over the mountain and ending up in

Las Vegas where they belong. There were times when, coming back from work, I just had to pack the family and flee to higher ground or toward the ocean for the evening, holding my breath as much as I could as I did so. Then measures were taken, some on the national and others on the local level. I complained when I had to install a catalytic converter on my car. I felt convinced paint would wash away when we were told to replace oil-based paints with water-based ones. I remember thinking the Air Quality Management District was really going too far when I read that small furniture makers, unable to buy the expensive equipment able to filter out the fumes from their varnishes, were moving out of the area. I never connected the bans with my real anxiety about air pollution because I never thought these small measures could really change anything. But over the years, I came to realize that I had not experienced any stage-four air pollution days for quite some time. I had not had to escape from the toxic brew. I was no longer thinking of permanently leaving the area. All those hundred different measures taken by the AQMD had had a profound effect: Los Angeles was livable again.

Using a vertical number line is like one of those many small measures that in themselves may not change much. There is no reason to implement them unless we have some belief that, ultimately, significant change is possible. If we allow some hope to creep in that the alienation from mathematics that so many students experience can be reversed, then the question changes from "Why bother?" to "Why not?" On its own, a vertical line will not reverse the absence in many students of the most elementary number sense that we see reflected in dismal statistics, but the alternative is essentially accepting that nothing much can be done about those statistics and the gaps they describe.

Using a vertical line as the accepted norm is something that might ultimately affect those statistics. It might contribute to doing so even if I do not really need it with my own students who may be doing quite well with the standard horizontal version. The changes that need to happen will not occur unless teachers take on goals that reach beyond their own students and their own classrooms.

Where I grew up, we never used a number line of any kind in our math classes. I discovered them when I came to America as an adult. They made a lot of sense. But not having been brought up in the American way of doing math, it was also easier for me to ask myself, as other have done, "Why horizontal? Why not vertical?" As I look at the changes I suggest in *Teaching to Intuition*, I do not think that I am often importing ideas or strategies from abroad. I do what all teachers do: I remain constantly attentive to the needs of my students and the difficulties they encounter, and I try to meet those needs. Not being born within the American tradition just makes it a little easier for me to look outside the box for solutions.

5

The Structure of the Four Operations

The four operations are the most fundamental topic in mathematics. Students early on learn the function of each operation. They learn essential facts such as $7 \times 7 = 49$ and traditional algorithms that allow them to multiply 348×729. They apply them to fractions and integers and other incarnations of numbers. The four operations are the fundamental building blocks of mathematics and deserve all the attention they can get. Delving into their structure facilitates our students' ability to build on their intuitive understanding.

The motivation for inventing operations in the first place is born of our need to add, subtract, multiply, or divide actual things. Mathematics then develops abstract relationships between numbers. The tools developed in the abstract are then applied once again to actual things. We learn to manipulate 5 and 7, but we no longer have 5 and 7 when we apply math to the real world. We have 5 dollars and 7 dollars or 5 students that have 7 dollars each. Not surprisingly, the logical requirements of numbers attached to real things inform abstract arithmetic. We discover the structure of the four operations as we look at numbers in context, attached to real "things," in the broadest sense of the word.

Addition and Subtraction

We attached numbers to real things when we introduced operations on fractions. We asked students three questions about cats and dogs. These questions used addition with numbers attached to familiar pets. This led to an understanding that we can only add and subtract things that have or have been given the same name. We helped students discover what they already knew intuitively and become aware of the strategy they used when trying to add things that had a different name: cats and dogs, brothers and sisters, girls and boys in a classroom, apples and oranges. We then turned to fractions and helped students discover that the logical structure that they had recognized in real life also requires a common denominator before we can add or subtract fractions.

Subsequently, students would discover that the same internal logic implies that we can only add "like terms" in algebra: I cannot add 5xy and 3xyz because I wouldn't know if I had 8xy or 8xyz. We can only add things that have "the same name," fractions that have a "common denominator," and "like terms" in algebra. "Name," "denominator," and "term" are three different words for the same reality. What students had discovered before we turned to fractions, as they attempted to add dogs and cats, was a first step in establishing the structure of the four operations.

When Mary at the checkout counter showed an intuitive understanding that we must multiply before we can add, she did so in the context of numbers attached to real things. She instinctively knew that "10 cans at $0.75 a can" must be transformed by multiplication into a single dollar amount before the number can be added to the dollar cost of her other purchases. So the requirement that multiplications must be done before additions and subtractions is another incarnation of the logical requirement that we can only add things that have the same name. This is an insight that completely escapes most of our students who, when considering a sequence of operations with numbers unattached to objects, are likely to accept the priority given to multiplication and division as an arbitrary rule of mathematics.

The notion of place value has many components. One also rests on the understanding that you can only add things that have the same name. I don't know many first graders who, having mastered orally "3 books + 5 books = 8 books" will not eagerly extend the knowledge to hundreds, thousands, and millions: "3 hundred + 5 hundred = 8 hundred"; "3 thousand + 5 thousand = 8 thousand." The correlation is not as obvious with numbers smaller than 100 because the most frequently used numbers enjoy the privilege of being the most irregular. The oral version of 30 + 50 does not reflect the structure as clearly as 300 + 500. But we can help students become familiar with the logic with hundreds, thousands, and millions and only then transfer the understanding to 30 and 50 or 13 and 5.

In short, the central characteristic of the structure of additions and subtractions, that we can only add or subtract things that have the same name, is likely to surface unexpectedly at many junctures in our exploration of mathematics.

Multiplication

With multiplication, $3 \times 7 = 7 \times 3$. The two factors have the same weight, the same importance. They are interchangeable. We even have a mathematical term for that feature: the commutative property of multiplication. We may also point out that the English language integrates that property in ways that other languages may not. "Three times five" can be understood as 3 times the number 5 or as the number 3 repeated 5 times. This ambiguity is not possible in French, for instance, where we have to choose between 3 times the number 5 and 5 times the number 3.

As we consider numbers attached to actual things, the commutative property essentially loses its significance. We no longer have two undifferentiated factors of equal importance: "*3 students* each put *7 books* on the table." If we multiply the two numbers, we get 21 books, not 21 students. In its most fundamental incarnation, multiplication is a shortcut for repeated addition of the same number. Here, the number that is added repeatedly is the number of books. Instead of adding 7 books + 7 books + 7 books, we decide to multiply 7 books by 3. The 3 students are just irrelevant embodiments for 3 groups. We still get 21 books if 3 teachers each bring 7 books—or 3 principals or 3 parcels received through the mail.

The structure of multiplication, in context, is this:

Number of items in each group
× *number of groups*
= Total *number of items*

In a multiplication word problem, the two number-words are different: *books* and *students* in our example, the word for the item that is being added repeatedly and the word for the group. The product is then attached to one of those words, the word for the items. The word for the group is often identified by the word "each" which conveys two notions: the notion of "one" (1 student brings 7 books) and the understanding that this characteristic of one group applies to all the groups.

With addition, we may have this:

"books ... books ... = books"

With multiplication, we have two different words:

"books ... students ... = books"

This is why addition and subtraction come before multiplication (and division). As our shoppers well know, we can only add dollars to dollars. We must wait until multiplication changes 10 cans at $0.75 a can into a single dollar amount ($7.50) before we can add.

And yet, when we seek to apply multiplication to this big, beautiful, infinitely varied world of ours, the words we use to describe the correlation between the abstractions of mathematics and practical reality find it difficult, even impossible, to adequately cover the diversity. We speak of the number of "items," but the word begins to unravel when the items we multiply become less tangible, such as thoughts or colors. "Repeated addition" loses some of its descriptive clarity when the "number of groups" is smaller than one. When we use multiplication to represent a difference in scale, or the number of possible combinations between different options, where are the items or the groups? At a certain level of sophistication it makes a lot of sense to use different classifications to describe and better understand those different circumstances.

And yet, under the apparent inconsistencies and the inadequacy of our vocabulary, we can still recognize the underlying pattern. When we multiply 5 cm by 3 to change the scale of a segment, we can still imagine the 5 cm measure repeated 3 times along the larger 15 cm segment: we have 3 groups with 5 centimeters in each group. When we combine 3 shapes and 7 colors to obtain 21 different combinations, we can still imagine 3 groups of shapes with 7 color options in each, or 7 groups of colors with 3 shape options in each for a total of 21 different options.

When we multiply 3 feet by 6 feet to find an area of 18 square feet, we have good reasons to focus on the exception to the general pattern of factors that represent two different realities with one of these number-words and the final product representing the same "item." We don't multiply cats and we certainly don't multiply cats to get dogs. But we can also consider that multiplying linear feet to get an area is a convenient substitute for thinking in terms of six foot-wide columns with three square-foot units in each group or three rows with six square-foot units in each.

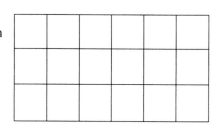

6 feet: 6 columns with
3 square feet in each: $6 \times 3 = 18$

3 feet: 3 rows with
6 square units in
each: $3 \times 6 = 18$

It just happens that the number of groups (the columns or the rows) and the number of square units in each group can both be formulated in terms of the linear measurements.

Division

Noticing the structure of multiplication is particularly useful as we turn to division.

Division undoes what multiplication does. We divide the product of the multiplication by one of the factors and get the other factor as the quotient of the division.

$3 \times 7 = 21$ So $21 \div 3 = 7$
$21 \div 7 = 3$

With numbers used in context, the perfect symmetry between the two options no longer applies.

71

3 books at 7 dollars each = 21 dollars

So   21 dollars ÷ 3 books = 7 dollars
               21 dollars ÷ 7 dollars = 3 books

Division undoes what multiplication does. Multiplication has two very different kinds of factors, so there are two very different kinds of divisions. One calculates the number of items in one group, the other the number of groups.

The more familiar is division as breaking up equally into a known number of groups:

I have $21.00. I want to buy 3 hamburgers. Division tells me I can spend $7.00 on each.

Let's call it the partitioning or *partitive* version.

        Total *number of items*
÷   *number of groups*
=   *number of items* in one group.

The other version calculates the number of groups:

I have $21.00. Each hamburger costs $7.00. Division tells me I can buy 3 hamburgers.

        Total *number of items*
÷   *number of items* (in one group)
=   *number of groups*.

If multiplication is repeat addition, this version of division can be understood as repeat subtraction. I can buy 1 hamburger, which leaves me with 14 dollars; and another one, and another one again. By the time I run out of money, I will have bought 3 hamburgers. I subtract one group of items over and over again and count how many times "7 dollars" goes into "21 dollars." (It is sometimes referred to as the "measurement" approach because of a frequent application to dividing two distances or two measures of weight or volume: "How many 3-ounce portions can you get from a 21-ounce dish?" This does not help students identify it in circumstances not strictly related to measurement.)

In mathematics unattached to things, we can decide which of the two interpretations to give to a division. In real life or word problems, we do not have that choice. The distinction is stark and can be seen from a distance, so to speak.

- *With the partitive version, the two number-words in the problem are different*: one stands for the total number of items and the other for the number of groups.
- *With the repeat subtraction version of division, the two number-words are the same:* one still stands for the total number of items, the other one stands for the number of items in each group.

We see reflected in the structure for the repeat subtraction model of division another manifestation of our old friend, the requirement that we can only add or subtract things that have the same name. Given 21 dollars, I can only subtract a number of dollars. Division

73

as repeat subtraction tells me how many times I can do this. Repeat subtraction can only occur when the two number-words in the formulation of the problem are the same.

Awareness of those two contrasting patterns is crucial in helping students recognize division word problems. The two kinds of divisions need to be learned, practiced, manipulated, and reviewed. Activities can help students contrast and practice those two versions of division.

For the partitive version, students can break up 21 tokens into 3 equal groups by making 3 piles of tokens of equal height. They find out that each pile has 7 tokens. Or they can take 21 cards and deal them out to 3 players. Each one ends up having 7 cards. They start with 21 items and some physical representation of the 3 groups, the 3 piles, or the 3 players.

To model the same division (21 ÷ 3 = 7), but with 21 and 3 representing the same object such as $21.00 used to buy $3.00 notebooks, students can use 3 fingers to subtract 3 tokens at a time from the 21 tokens and find out that they can do this 7 times. The three tokens subtracted at the same time represent the three items in each group.

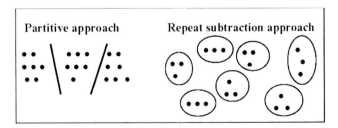

By practicing the two kinds of divisions in different ways, by reflecting each time we have a division word problem on the meaning of the division, and by seeing this meaning confirmed by number-words in the problem that are either different or similar, we are building in the minds of our students patterns that will lead to an intuitive recognition of which operation to perform.

Without the mental pattern, repeat subtraction division problems can be difficult to identify. Let's look at the model solution offered by a widely used textbook.

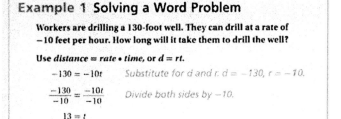

Example 1 Solving a Word Problem

Workers are drilling a 130-foot well. They can drill at a rate of −10 feet per hour. How long will it take them to drill the well?

Use *distance = rate • time*, or *d = rt.*

$$-130 = -10t \qquad \text{Substitute for d and r. } d = -130, r = -10.$$

$$\frac{-130}{-10} = \frac{-10t}{-10} \qquad \text{Divide both sides by } -10.$$

$$13 = t$$

It takes 13 hours to drill the well.

Holt. *Algebra Readiness.* (California edition, p. 449.)

Here, a memorized formula (d = rt) and mechanical substitution replace the most basic form of understanding. Division is one of the four basic operations. If students need to rely on the time/distance formula to solve this problem instead of immediately and intuitively identifying a division problem, then we have in effect given up expecting students to use mathematical knowledge to make sense of the world they live in. The artificial substitution of a memorized formula is the complete opposite of what we try to achieve in *Teaching to Intuition*. The alternative is to help students acquire in their minds a clear and compelling pattern of the repeat subtraction version of division.

> With real-life or word problems solved by dividing, we do not have a choice: either the two number-words are different (and we have a partitive approach to division), or the two number-words are the same (and we have a repeat subtraction problem).

With a division in the abstract, we have the choice of which interpretation to give to the division. Often the partitive approach is the easier for student to visualize but not always.

When dividing small numbers, students may find it convenient to use repeat subtraction, for instance when changing an improper fraction into a mixed number:

$\underline{25}$ Students can keep track with their fingers:
7 7... 14 ... 21. (That's 3.)

They can use the other hand to keep track of the fractional part: 22 ... 23 ... 24 ... 25. (That's 4.) Thus, 25/7 is 3 and 4/7. It takes learning and some practice, but it is a convenient approach and helps students experience division as repeat subtraction.

Dividing into a fractional number of parts is difficult to conceptualize. With fractions or numbers smaller than 1, the repeat subtraction approach is often the easier one to picture in our mind and the easier one to use to form an estimate of the magnitude of the answer.

Here, we begin by using simple whole numbers to remind students of the repeat subtraction meaning of division:

$15 \div 5 = 3$ How many times does 5 go into 15?
The answer is 3 times.

Students give their assent to this interpretation of division, and we then transfer the understanding to fractions:

$7/8 \div 2/7$ How many times does 2/7 go into 7/8?

Let us count: "2/7 ... 4/7 ... 6/7." 6/7 is still slightly smaller than 7/8 (1/7, not 1/8, smaller than 1). So the quotient is slightly greater than 3.

The procedural algorithm gives the actual value, but we can imagine most divisions of fractions performed by the whole class preceded by an estimate of the magnitude of the answer or followed by a check on the answer through some form of mental calculation, answering the question, does our answer make sense? Here, once again, the repeat subtraction interpretation may help.

Our concern with the structure of the four operations has led us to many different places—from a justification of the rules for adding fractions or algebraic terms, to a justification for multiplying or dividing before adding or subtracting, to some confirmation of the logic of place value and a suggestion to use hundreds and thousands to experience its logic before returning to smaller numbers, to an option for dividing small numbers and an approach that allows us to give meaning to division by a fraction. Perhaps most importantly, it allows us to communicate to our students a clear distinction between two forms of division and how to easily identify one from the other, leaving them with a crucial mental pattern that is often found lacking. This builds connections, categories, and structures in the mind that can then be used to make sense of other mathematical procedures and of the outside world in mathematical terms.

In teaching to intuition, we are not satisfied with presenting each aspect of such broad topics as individual truths. On this and other topics, we want students to acquire the broad picture and to see connections between very different incarnations of the same mathematical truths.

Intuition, then, occurs when we recognize in new circumstances or new problems an echo of familiar patterns, categories, and understandings that are already in our minds.

6

The Order of Operations

A frequent approach to teaching the order of operations is through a mnemonic device, an acronym such as "Please Excuse My Dear Aunt Sally."

The initial letters of the words (PEMDAS) remind students of the order of operations: Parentheses, Exponents, Multiplication, Division, Addition, Subtraction. Though sometimes convenient, mnemonic devices such as this one are by their very nature almost the complete opposite of what we try to achieve by teaching to intuition.

> In this case, the real harm is done when the mnemonic device puts the four basic operations on a continuum: multiplications, then divisions, then additions, then subtractions. First, it is not true. There is no absolute obligation to add before we subtract or to multiply before we divide. Then, it leaves students with only a vague notion that multiplication and division are one category, almost a slightly different version of the same operation, and addition and subtraction another contrasting category. Entrusting the knowledge to the mnemonic fails to anchor those two levels of operations in our students' minds.

Students pay the price later. That contrast could throw a powerful clarifying light on the rules and procedures for operations on fractions and integers. Without the mental structure of those two levels of operations, everything tends to be confused. I put considerable blame for this confusion on the dear lady. So I am about to be very cruel. She may be family, but in my eyes, she has run out of excuses. I would like to march My Dear Aunt Sally out of her cell, stand her up against a wall, and call in the firing squad. She has done enough harm already. On second thought, this may be a little severe. A good lawyer might secure a lighter sentence, arguing that the real harm doesn't come from what the mnemonic says but from what it almost inevitably allows many students not to learn and experience. But in an emergency, we may skip the subtleties.

So what can be done about the order of operations? Let's take each initial from the mnemonic in turn.

P is for Parentheses

Parentheses are a very graphic symbol. It should not be difficult to communicate to students an understanding that what's inside parentheses is in its own little world. The operations inside need to be done first.

But more needs to be taught and understood about parentheses.

1. Their primary use is to disrupt what would otherwise be the regular order of operations:

   $$7 + 5 \times 10 + 6$$
   $$= \quad 7 + \quad 50 \quad + 6 \qquad = \qquad 63$$

   Parentheses can change this:

   $$(7 + 5) \times (10 + 6)$$
   $$= \quad 12 \quad \times \quad 16 \qquad = \qquad 192$$

2. Parentheses can also be used to highlight the regular order of operations without changing it:

   $(3 \times 9) + (5 \times 3)$ is clearer but no different from $3 \times 9 + 5 \times 3$.

Like all languages, mathematics has obligations that go beyond its abstract accuracy. Clarity in communicating that accuracy to others has its importance. A habit of adding parentheses in this way can help bring clarity to ourselves as well as to others. Rather than just asking students to correctly evaluate expressions that include additions/subtractions and multiplications/divisions, I would suggest we ask students to show them first with those optional parentheses.

3. It often helps to think of everything inside parentheses as a single number or a single variable and to treat it as such. All the manipulations that bear on numbers and variables remain valid when the quantity they represented is an expression inside parentheses.

The Common Core State Standards for Mathematical Practice encourage students to develop their ability to see parts of expressions as separate identities. They are encouraged "to see complicated things, such as some algebraic expressions, as single objects or as being composed of several objects." The judicious use of optional parentheses can help develop that ability.

4. Students can be shown other symbols or formats that act like parentheses. For instance, everything that is on one side or the other of the equal sign can be seen as inside virtual parentheses and as such can be treated like a single number; or everything above or below a fraction bar.

5. Finally, students can be helped to see in the procedures of the distributive property a tool to break through the cozy isolation created by parentheses. In particular, it becomes impossible to evaluate the content of parentheses if one of the terms is a variable. Applying the distributive property offers an alternative.

Parentheses are a clear visual signal that they identify entities that belong together, entities that it makes eminent sense to evaluate separately, when possible, before including them in a sequence of operations. That message is so clear that students can leave parentheses out of what they need to learn about the order of operations. They can focus instead on what they really need to know on the subject. Just putting parentheses at the beginning of the list of priorities should not substitute for a well-developed examination of the role of parentheses, real or imagined.

E is for Exponent

When we think of a number, it is easy to imagine 0.75 or 169. But a number is not just a number when written in the usual format. It remains a single number even when written using two or more numbers. In particular, a single number can be written as a fraction, a root, in scientific notation, or as a power of any other number. The numbers 0.75 and 169 can be written as 3/4 and 13^2. It makes sense to think of an exponent as really one part of a single number. It doesn't make sense to even envisage splitting up base and exponent. In $5x^2y^4z^3$, each variable is a base raised individually to a given power. In $5xyz^2$, knowing that exponent comes before multiplication doesn't of itself fully resolve the possible difficulty in identifying the base, though it does help conclude that you can't just do each of the operations in the order in which the numbers are written. A memorized jingle does not fully substitute for a more fundamental understanding.

My Dear Aunt Sally

The four remaining initials are for the four essential operations. The mnemonic device seems to imply an absolute priority of multiplication over division and of addition over subtraction. It doesn't distinguish the essential contrast between the first two (multiplication and division) and the other two (addition and subtraction). Instead, I would stress the notion of hierarchy. Multiplications and divisions each represent a number of additions or subtractions and are more important than individual additions or subtractions. But the real understanding for giving priority to multiplication and division over addition and subtraction comes from looking at the numbers attached to real things or by looking at a sales slip from a supermarket and observing how giving priority to multiplication allows us to add dollars to dollars instead of adding cans and dollars, which makes no sense.

In short, though students need to evaluate parentheses and raise bases to the powers of their exponents before including these numbers in other calculations, I would entrust that knowledge to a more intimate understanding of these requirements. Under the rubric "order of operations," I would be satisfied to include only the four basic operations and imply essentially a distinction between two sets of operations, two levels of hierarchy:

> Multiplication and divisions are done first.
> Additions and subtractions come last.

My major objection to the mnemonic is not in terms of the order of operations. It is because of what happens some grades later, as a response to seeing students who do not have firmly established in their minds the contrast between these two levels of operations and who, when learning about operations on fractions and on integers, do not have the two crucial mental categories that they need if they are to make sense of the rules and procedures. As we seek to teach to intuition, we open our imagination to the importance of such mental patterns and categories, on the vision they allow students to have of a set of rules or the mushy confusion that occurs when such categories are not prominent patterns in their minds. By using the short-term mnemonic, we are depriving students of the best opportunity they have of acquiring a strong mental picture of the contrast between those two levels of operations.

7

Formulas

Because it seeks to tweak not just how we teach but what it means to know, teaching to intuition affects in ways large or small just about everything that is taught in elementary and middle school mathematics. For each topic, the response is different. We have examined so far strategies that affect numbers and operations. Let's turn to formulas, in particular as they are used in geometry.

Anything that traditionally relies mostly on memory needs to be examined carefully. Pure memorization is knowledge that we draw from outside ourselves, knowledge that we retain on the authority of the teacher or a textbook. It is also knowledge that is easy to forget. The cumulative effect of more and more material committed to memory or that slips through the net of memory builds ever larger gaps and challenges. These gaps make it even more difficult to learn new material. Math becomes a confusing mass of rules and regulations. Frustration increases. Egos are bruised repeatedly in small ways that freeze into a deep resentment and a deep aversion to things mathematical.

When asking students to commit to memory, we need to ask ourselves, is it really the only option? Sometimes, it may be. But alternatives to just memorizing are likely to exist. They can help build connections and understanding—and ultimately unleash creativity. A constant effort to lighten the burden of memorization is a crucial dimension of teaching to intuition.

One of my early surprises as I became acquainted through my children's homework to the American approach to teaching math was when I realized that they were being asked to know a formula for the perimeter of a rectangle. $P = 2l + 2w$ seemed to be the choice. Why two multiplications and an addition was better at that early level than the three additions required if the child's finger was allowed to move around the perimeter of a rectangle or the single addition and single multiplication of $P = 2(l + w)$ is still a mystery. But essentially, the requirement is an invitation for students to substitute memorization for understanding. It allows some, gradually, to remember the formula and forget about the meaning of perimeter. Even worse, perhaps, it allows students who know the meaning to forget that the simplest thinking process can yield the value. "What's the perimeter of this rectangle?" "I don't know. What's the formula?" It is difficult to find a clearer example of what can be terribly wrong in a child's attitude toward math. Instead of being understood as an activity of the brain, mathematics is embodied here in knowing a formula. When a formula is finally needed, for instance to solve a problem in algebra, then there should be no difficulty in re-creating one. This is the least we can expect of students who learn to use mathematics to model the world.

We saw another example of a memorized formula used as a substitute to the most basic understanding earlier in the model solution offered by a textbook to a word problem about digging a well. There is hope that the Common Core State Standards' insistence on understanding and modeling will eliminate such practices.

So how do we deal with formulas? There is no single answer. We may re-create them, teach them, make them easier to remember by discovering connections, or simply do without them.

Establishing Connections

Tired of seeing students multiply two sides of a triangle or parallelogram to find the area, we can tell them that finding an area, for them, consists in always multiplying two perpendicular distances.

With the help of visual props, we can show that just knowing two sides of a parallelogram gives us figures with very different areas. We can squeeze a rectangle made of drinking straws to just about nothing without changing the length of the sides.

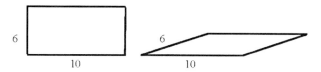

"6 x 10 = 60 square units. Can this be the area of both figures?"

If the same lengths can produce different areas, logic implies that we cannot know the area from knowledge of the two sides alone. There is no area to find unless we have some extra piece of information, some additional constraint. So we tell students that, to find an area, they need to "multiply two perpendicular distances." Each word here is important, with an emphasis on the word *perpendicular* that provides the extra constraint. A gesture of the hands, one open hand perpendicular to the open palm of the other hand, gives a visual dimension to the injunction.

When we multiply two perpendicular distances, we get the area of a rectangle. That area often needs to be modified to fit the figure at hand. For instance, in the case of triangles, the area of the rectangle obtained by multiplying base and height needs to be divided by 2 to find the area of the triangle.

> The instruction to multiply two perpendicular distances creates a link, a *connection*, between all the area formulas normally considered in elementary and middle school. It is a unifying pattern that overcomes the isolation of the separate formulas and provides some strategy for eliminating wrong approaches and for remembering or re-creating the correct formula. It helps shift the knowledge away from pure memorization. It allows students to ask themselves, "What two perpendicular distances am I going to multiply?" It reflects an understanding of what is achieved by multiplying.

Students can be helped to identify the two perpendicular distances, to visualize the corresponding rectangle (here shown as a dotted line for a triangle and a circle), and to understand why and by what factor its area needs to be modified.[*]

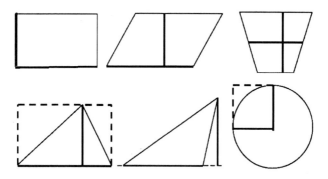

We can then use the injunction ourselves to prompt students struggling to remember a formula. It can be a simple gesture of the hands (one hand perpendicular to the palm of the other) directed at a student who multiplies two nonperpendicular sides of a triangle.

It can be asking: Which two perpendicular distances are you going to multiply?

---

[*] Multiplying two perpendicular distances applies to all areas students normally consider at this level, including the circle. However, it is not a rule of mathematics. The triangle is an exception. If we know the three sides, we have a unique triangle with a unique area. It cannot be squeezed into a different shape with a different area. That's why triangles are so important in building bridges or other rigid structures. If three nonperpendicular sides define a triangle with a unique area, count on mathematicians to find a way of calculating that area from knowledge of the three sides. That's where Hero's formula comes in.

Or commenting:	Good. You just multiplied two perpendicular distances. That gives you the area of a rectangle. Show me that rectangle. What else do you need to do?

These "five-second review" strategies direct students back to the understanding or the mental patterns that allow them to recreate the formula.

In the same perspective, we will tell students that, to find a volume, they will always multiply *three perpendicular distances*. Of course, two of these distances can be represented by an area.

Area and Circumference of a Circle

The formulas for the circumference and area of a circle are crucial. As such, we can't just ask students to commit them to memory. They need to be taught.

Let's say that we have chosen the formulas for the circumference and the area in terms of the radius:

$$C = 2\pi r \qquad\qquad A = \pi r^2$$

Both $2\pi r$ and πr^2 use the same three numbers or variables. This can be an extra difficulty for our students who may mix up the formulas, or we can change it into an opportunity. I want my students to notice that the same three characters are used: 2, π, and r. It's obvious, but students still need help to notice it. If they don't, confusion arises as they extract the formulas from their memories and only then notice the resemblance and no longer remember which is which.

Then, I reach out for help to what my students have learned about multiplying two perpendicular distances to find an area, though the perpendicular component is not immediately needed:

> If you were given the two formulas and didn't know which was for the circumference and which for the area, how could you tell?

> Which variable represents a distance?

> In which formula do you multiply a distance by a distance?

πr^2 is a formula for an area; $2\pi r$ is not. The connecting link we provided for area formulas helps students discriminate between the formulas for area and circumference.

Now let's teach the two formulas. Here is an option.

Teacher takes three sheets of paper and cuts a few 1/2 inch strips. Each strip is three sheets thick. Going around the classroom with the strips, the teacher cuts 1/2 inch lengths of strip for each student. One clip of the scissors and students have three small 1/2 inch squares of paper. On each, they write one of the characters: 2, π, r. Students are then asked to arrange the small squares to show the formula for the circumference and to rearrange the squares to show the formula for the area of a circle.

Answers are checked. Some students need to be helped to really show 2 as an exponent.

When students know this well, the teacher moves on to the next topic, a topic that may have nothing to do with circles or even mathematics. But then, a number of times during the next hour or day, the topic at hand is interrupted. Students are asked to go back to their squares and arrange them as either the formula for the circumference or the area. Quick check. Quick reminder of why r^2 goes with the area.

The point is that, once it has been established that they are needed, formulas can be taught. Here, teaching implies creating links and contrasts between the two formulas and also a link with the general understanding that we multiply two distances to find an area.

Circles and Spheres: Formulas and Patterns

Let's look at the injunction to multiply two perpendicular distances to find an area as it applies to the circle, $A = \pi r^2$. The two perpendicular distances are two radii. The rectangle defined by r^2 is a square with a radius as its side. It is one quarter of the large square circumscribed to the circle which has $(2r)^2$ or $4r^2$ as its area.

The area of the inscribed circle is smaller than $4r^2$. We get that area by replacing 4 with 3.14 or π. The ratio between the areas of a square and that of its inscribed circle is 4 to π.

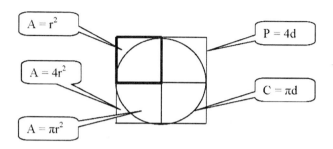

That relationship has its use in real life. To control the amount of water used or available, firemen often need to know the area of a cross section of a hose or the volume of a cylindrical water tank. This implies finding the area of a circle. Every second counts. The diameter is the easiest of the dimensions to measure. The formulas firemen are taught uses diameter D and the constant $\pi/4$ (0.7854) as more convenient than π alone: $A = .7854D^2$ for the cross-sectional area of a fire hose; $V = .7854D^2h$ for the volume of water in a cylindrical tank, the area of the base times the height.

Interestingly, the ratio of the perimeter of a square to the circumference of the inscribed circle is also 4 to π. So if we compare a square to its inscribed circle, both for the perimeter/circumference and for the area, the ratio is 4 to π. Unless you are a fireman trying to make sense of the apparent discrepancy between formulas learned in school and those learned in firefighting classes, this observation is not very useful in itself, but it raises a question about the cube and its inscribed sphere. Is it possible? Could it be as simple as that? Well, it is.

> The square has 4 sides.
> The ratio between square and inscribed circle, both for perimeter and area, is 4 to π.

> The cube has 6 sides.
> The ratio between cube and inscribed sphere, both for the surface area and for the volume, is 6 to π.

With this observation, students and the adults they become have immediate access to the surface area and volume of the sphere, provided that they know how to calculate the surface area and volume of a cube.

If D is the diameter of a sphere, the corresponding cube has a volume of D^3 which can be written as $6D^3/6$. So the volume of the sphere is $\pi D^3/6$, which can be written in terms of the radius as $4\pi r^3/3$.

A cube has 6 sides. Its surface area is $6D^2$. So the surface area of the sphere is πD^2. These two observations are likely to have a significantly longer shelf life than memorized formulas.

Checking on Memorized Formulas

Students can also be equipped with simple strategies for checking on formulas they are asked to memorize. A student thinks she remembers the formula for the difference of two squares: $a^2 - b^2 = (a + b)(a - b)$. It doesn't take long to verify, either by using the distributive property to expand $(a + b)(a - b)$, or by checking that it works for $a = 6$ and $b = 2$, for instance. The strategy needs to be taught and practiced. Even as we ask students to memorize, students need to learn that they are not always left helpless at the mercy of their memories.

8

The Common Core State Standards

At this stage of mathematical education in the United States, the Common Core State Standards (CCSS) adopted by a majority of states represent the most likely opportunity for bringing about change. It could even be dramatic change, the kind of change that is needed to lift the country out of its multilevel achievement gaps in mathematics and turn it away from a practice of math that, in the words of the standards, is "a mile wide and an inch deep." But it is not a given that they will do so. Deep-seated habits of mind and practices are difficult to change. And even as they formulate general expectation for a significant change and provide some guidance in that direction, the standards themselves are not immune to the habits of mind that could prevent the change from happening. So let's take their goals seriously, seriously enough to disagree on occasion with the means they suggest.

The Common Core State Standards in Mathematics give two sets of directives: the content standards and the standards for practice. They also include an introduction and supporting documentation.

The grade-specific Standards for *Content* describe the math that needs to be learned at the various stages of a student's studies. These are generally fewer, more focused, and probably more rigorous than previous state standards. Also, they should make it easier for students to adjust even if they change schools, districts, or states.

The Standards for *Practice* state that students should be able to "apply the mathematics they know to solve problems arising in everyday life, society, and the workplace." In other words, the Standards for *Practice* define the purpose of the knowledge defined by the *Content* Standards. The Standards for Practice list the skills, tools, and circumstances that make this possible in terms that apply to all levels.

This emphasis on practice, on using math to model the world we live in and on communicating one's knowledge to others, is perhaps the most significant change brought about by the Common Core State Standards.

> That new emphasis on practice, on using math to model the outside world, is valuable and commendable in itself, but it also reflects back on the content knowledge and how it is learned. A procedural approach to knowing content is incompatible with the flexibility and creativity needed as we seek to apply that knowledge to the real world. The standards are clear on the issue: "A lack of understanding *effectively prevents* a student from engaging in the mathematical practices." (Emphasis added.)

In the introduction and supporting documentation, the Common Core State Standards contrast *procedures* and *understanding*, and without ruling out mastery of procedures, they see a danger in the mechanical pursuit of procedures devoid of understanding. The supporting presentation states, "Students who lack understanding of a topic may rely on procedures too heavily."

They quote from "established research":

> Because the mathematics concepts in [US] textbooks are often weak, the presentation becomes more mechanical than is ideal.

Mnemonic Device

In expanding on "understanding mathematics," the standards choose as an illustration the use of a mnemonic often used in beginning algebra. Let us quote this:

> There is a world of difference between the student who can summon a mnemonic device to expand a product such as $(a + b)(x + y)$ and a student who can explain where the mnemonic comes from. The student who can explain the rule understands the mathematics and may have a better chance to succeed at a less familiar task such as expanding $(a + b + c)(x + y)$.

The mnemonic device they refer to is FOIL (First, Outer, Inner, Last). It shows the different combinations needed to multiply $(a + b)(x + y)$ or similar binomials into the expanded product $(ax + ay + bx + by)$. It is no different from having to distribute 5 colored pencils and

101

7 sheets of paper to each student in two classes, one with 10 students, and the other with 12. There is a need for 5 pencils each for 10 students, 7 sheets for 10 students, 5 pencils for 12 students, and 7 sheets for 12 students; otherwise the students in one of the classrooms might not get their pencils or their paper. Not surprisingly, the algebraic rule that reflects that reality is called the *distributive* property.

The alternative to memorizing FOIL is an understanding that each term in the first bracket is distributed in turn to each term in the second. That understanding applies to distributing any number of objects to any number of classes, not just two.

For instance, with $(a - b)(x - y + z)$ we are showing the algebraic equivalent of distributing to or collecting from three entities of one kind or another. The quote from the standards points out that, without understanding, the purely mechanic mnemonic is powerless to expand beyond binomials.

Let's imagine demonstrating graphically the process in a way that reflects the understanding. We may begin by drawing a bubble around variable a and multiplying it with each term in the second bracket. We then do the same with the second variable in the second bubble. We end up with the following diagram:

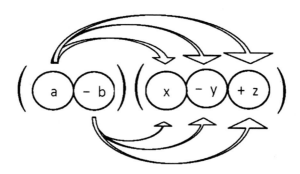

As students subsequently do so themselves, one variable and one connecting arrow at a time, they establish a strong connection between the procedure and its name: the *distributive* property, or, to give it its full name, the *distributive property of multiplication over addition and subtraction*. Beginning first with binomials, students learn and practice the basic discipline and organizational skills that allow them to systematically combine the terms through multiplication. It is not asking too much of students that are deemed ready to begin studying the abstract formulations of algebra.

By initially putting bubbles around the variables or numbers and the operation sign in front of them, we help students visualize the full scope of what is being multiplied: not just a number but whether the number is added or subtracted. The arrows model the understanding that each term within one set of parentheses needs to be multiplied by each term in the other. In the process, students acquire the experience of a pattern that can be generalized to multiplying any two polynomials, and also to multiplying a polynomial by a single term, such as a(x + y), or even of making sense of

103

a − (x − y + z), where the operation is distributed to all the terms within the parentheses.

In time, within the wide reach of the distributive property, the understanding allows students to recognize the pattern as it is reflected in explanations, illustrations, representations, and applications, both to other mathematical processes and to real-life situations. These include understanding that the algorithm for multiplication, where every digit of one of the factors is combined with every digit of the other factor, is just one application of the same property, of the same internal logic. The traditional multiplication algorithm for 354 × 917 is just a convenient way of applying the distributive property to (300 + 50 + 4)(900 + 10 + 7).

In short, conceptual understanding encouraged by the standards could contribute to building, over time, a rich and expanding network of connections.

In contrast, the mnemonic FOIL (which the standards refer to but do not name) is an empty shell that can be applied to binomial in the absence of any understanding. It is purely procedural, purely mechanical. It focuses exclusively on an immediate need and robs student of the long-term benefits of meeting that need through understanding. As the standards point out, it does not prepare students for the obvious next step as they move beyond binomials to slightly more advanced levels of algebra. It contributes nothing to the rich web of connections and patterns that must be a characteristic of mathematical thinking if students are to acquire the creativity and flexibility implied by the Common Core Standard for Mathematical Practice.

In any one classroom, it is possible for students to fully understand the distributive property and to still use FOIL to save a few seconds when dealing with binomials. But that is the shiny face of FOIL. It is not its real purpose. This is not why it is so widely used. FOIL, like so many other shortcuts that pervade the teaching of mathematics in the United States, is used by our weaker students as an alternative to understanding.

Faced with the challenge of teaching all students to multiply binomials, teachers have a choice: develop teaching strategies that will communicate the understanding to all their students and allow them to practice not just a procedure but the understanding itself, or find some stopgap alternative to understanding that meets the immediate need. Our weaker students, those that we most want not to leave behind, are the ones who are most helped by FOIL in the short term. They are also those who are most hurt by using it if the goal is to help them understand the distributive property, use it later to multiply any two polynomials, and recognize where it applies in the real world we want them to model with the tool of mathematics. They are the ones who most need the systematic practice of the discipline and organizational skills that reflect and implement the understanding.

In that perspective, using FOIL is not significantly different from using a formula to help students calculate the perimeter of a rectangle or offering the time/distance formula as a model solution for a simple division problem about digging a 130-foot well at a rate of 10 feet per hour. These are all short-term fixes that, in effect, allow students to circumvent the understanding.

But then, having selected FOIL to make a point, the standards fall short of providing a remedy that has any chance of reversing long-held practices. They want students "who can explain where the mnemonic comes from. The student who can explain the rule understands the mathematics." By setting up as a goal students "who can explain where the mnemonic comes from," the standards validate the use of the mnemonic. Worse still, in the same paragraph where FOIL is used as an illustration of the mechanical substituting itself to understanding, they specify, "Asking a student to understand something means asking a teacher to assess whether the student has understood it." So the standards specifically invite curriculum developers to design tests that test students on their understanding of FOIL, thus in effect preventing teachers who want to completely bypass the use of such devices from doing so. They are encouraging, almost requiring, the creation of those hundred small impediments that prevent teachers from fully teaching to their students' understanding.

Teachers already explain FOIL when it is initially presented. The timid admonition that students should understand it is unlikely to change much in what is already being done. It does not forcefully propose to teachers and curriculum developers a vision that understanding can become the central component of the knowledge. Instead, on this and other topics, teachers could be encouraged to trust that understanding, to develop strategies that allow them to do so, to see in it the road to more engaged students, to fewer students discouraged, left behind, or dropping out, and essentially to an easier teaching experience and significantly better results. Without necessarily banning FOIL (that is not their role, though it is a choice that I would hope many teachers would make), the standards should make it clear that any *reliance* on FOIL becomes a substitute for understanding. They should certainly not make it impossible for teachers to completely do without.

What the standards fail to communicate—perhaps what they fail to understand—is the magnitude of the change that is needed if long-held habits of mind are going to change.

> We can think of two approaches to mathematical knowledge. For some of our students, math is an accumulation of mnemonics such as FOIL, of memorized rules, and dry and essentially meaningless procedures, where each additional step adds its extra burden of complexity and confusion. For others, learning math is an expanding network of connections that enlighten and strengthen each other. For them, each new step is a door that opens to new possibilities, adding new dimensions to the knowledge and habits of mind already acquired.

Our more mathematically inclined students choose that approach on their own. Others need all our help and careful strategies to avoid falling into the mechanical, procedural approach that can only lead to frustration and ultimate failure. Even if it was mastered, the procedural approach would be useless, as it cannot help students reach out to the real world of practice. Real-life situations that we would like to understand with the help of mathematical modeling do not come with abstract mathematical terms pinned to them or with the mathematical name for an operation or property attached to them. Without understanding, the connection will not take place. The student will not recognize the need to dig a 130-foot well at 10 feet per hour as a situation that can be clarified by division.

As we teach math, the mental habits and expectations of our students are built one brick at a time, each one either fostering understanding and broadening the network of connections or adding to the accumulation of isolated facts and confirming a procedural approach. A number of times in each of our lessons, we can choose one or the other, or we can allow the choice to be made for us by our own habits of mind, our unquestioning acceptance of traditional approaches, or by our submission to choices made by a textbook or others. The teachers I meet yearn to teach to their students' understanding. They do so in any number of creative ways even as so much seems to stand in their way. I hope that *Teaching to Intuition* will empower those teachers to follow and defend their instincts and confirm them in their determination to do so.

The Properties of Operations

As can be expected, one of the priorities in the early grades is to master the basic addition and subtraction math facts and develop the ability to add and subtract. In contrast to earlier standards that simply instructed children to "commit to memory" addition and subtraction facts, the content standards of the CCSS encourage the use of mental strategies. They do so in particular in first-grade standard Operations and Algebraic Thinking (OA) No. 6. Those strategies are not just approaches that teach children how to memorize facts, they are strategies that students and the adults they become can rely on as a substitute to pure memorization.

This is extremely encouraging. Some students, even mathematically gifted ones, will never find it possible to master automatic recall for over three hundred combinations of addition and subtraction facts with sums no greater than 20. Valuable teaching time can be wasted trying to make them do so. As an alternative to pure memorization, students can follow the guideline of the standards and learn thinking strategies that help them rely on "equivalent but easier or known facts."

Standard 1.OA.6 refers in particular to strategies built on decomposing a number and using benchmarks. To add 8 + 6, the mind sees 8 as 2 units short of 10 and decomposes 6 into 2 and 4. The mind then adds 8 + 2 to make 10 and then adds 10 + 4. To add 6 + 7, the mind changes the problem to 6 + 6 + 1, doubles 6 and adds 1. These are two examples listed in the standards as just a sampling of what can be done. This might appear complicated to those lucky enough to have committed all the facts to pure memory, but it is not. It is also not a bad introduction to a habit of mind of using mental math and very simple mental strategies in real life—as we shop and want to compare prices, for instance.

So the approach focuses initially on a careful selection of "easier facts," and then on mental strategies that build on those facts. It is very much what we tried to do in a first-grade class with the itsy-bitsy spider and its waterspout. It stands in contrast to a blanket approach to learning math facts where all facts are given equal importance and drilled and practiced indiscriminately.

Thinking strategies for knowing facts need not fully substitute for efforts to help students memorize. The two approaches complement each other. The blend of pure memorization and thinking strategies will be different for every student. But the shift in emphasis away from pure memorization and endless repetitions is very welcome. I hope teachers and curriculum developers fully exploit and implement the approach. I hope they build on similar strategies for teaching multiplication as I have attempted to do in my *Making Friends with Numbers* collection of multiplication math fact work sheets.

Here again, however, the standards fail to follow through. They include a second set of strategies for learning how to add and subtract based on the commutative and associative properties of operations. It is stated and illustrated in this first-grade standard:

> *Apply properties of operations as strategies to add and subtract.* Examples: If $8 + 3 = 11$ is known, then $3 + 8 = 11$ is also known (commutative property of addition). To add $2 + 6 + 4$, the second two numbers can be added to make a ten, so $2 + 6 + 4 = 2 + 10 = 12$ (associative property of addition). (Standard 1.OA.3.)

The approach is selected a second time for first grade in the "Number and Operations" strand.

> Use place value understanding and properties of operations to add and subtract.

We find it in the second-grade standards.

> Apply properties of operations as strategies to add and subtract.

Third- and fourth-grade standards continue on the same theme.

> Use place value understanding and properties of operations to perform multidigit arithmetic.

Fifth-grade standards expand on the same injunction, suggesting the use of

> strategies based on place value, properties of operations, and/or the relationship between addition and subtraction.

I hear a broken record. I too want students who know that "if $8 + 3 = 11$ is known, then $3 + 8 = 11$ is also known." I too want students who know that if $8 + 3 = 11$ is known, then $11 - 3 = 8$ is also known. I hope they do so long before fifth grade.

As we watched shoppers at the checkout counter of a supermarket in our initial section, we saw the great facility they demonstrated in practice to move numbers around and group them in a series of additions and subtractions. We helped our students claim that same facility for formal mathematics and use the understanding as strategies for adding and subtracting. We saw how it stood in contrast to relying on properties of operations and expressed the hope that our students could use mental strategies without having to pay tribute to the troll of the commutative or associative properties hiding under the bridge. It seems that the Common Core State Standards want a troll lurking behind every tree.

There is absolutely no reason to put those two properties of addition in charge of the combinations and groupings that children are encouraged to imagine. Relying on those properties not only excludes combinations that involve subtraction but tends to imply that $5 + 2 = 2 + 5$ *because* of the commutative property of addition. The requirement to justify each move by some property disturbs and overwhelms the intimate knowledge of the facts, like a big stamp that proclaims:

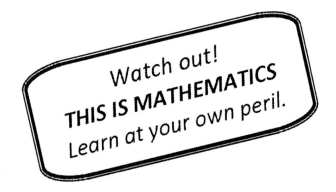

The overwhelming importance given to such technical relationships as those two properties could crowd out in the mind of teachers the full range of much more creative thinking strategies mentioned, but much more discreetly, by the Standards. I am concerned that teachers will feel compelled to justify some of these other strategies in terms of properties of operations as if the facts themselves were not knowledge enough, preventing students, for instance, from changing $2 + 6 + 4$ into $2 + 10$ without processing the change in terms of the associative property. I am concerned that teachers and curriculum developers will feel required or entitled to teach and test for the names of these properties despite a footnote that makes using the technical names optional. If that should happen, I hope teachers and parents will forcefully object, as that would impose on teachers an obligation to teach what is essentially counterproductive, what we earlier labeled as unlearning and unteaching, and what a footnote clearly establishes as optional.

Pedagogy is concerned with much more than the objective facts. It is affected by the emphasis, the context, and the implications. What we teach is molded by the unconscious pressures of our assumptions and beliefs. I fail to see how a teacher can be subjected to the massive emphasis on the commutative property demonstrated by the standard and still be satisfied with allowing children to take for granted that $2 + 3 = 3 + 2$.

As a teacher, I listen to my own mind as I teach. I ask myself if the explanations I give my students are those that I use to explain the material to myself, and if not, why not? So I had to ask myself what allowed the shoppers' perspective to be so much more powerful and liberating than the standards' emphasis on these two properties. As I asked myself the question, I came up with some unexpected answers. At the cost of some repetition, let me try to sort it out.

The Unitary Perspective

At its heart, it seems to me, the discrepancy between the two approaches is related to the binary nature of operations. As human beings, we are subjected to the constraint of time—not the lack of it, though teachers experience that too, but its passage, its linear and sequential flow. Operations fully assume that constraint as they refer to an action that we take. They are performed two numbers at a time. We add two numbers, then a third number to the sum, and a fourth to the new total, and so on. All four operations are binary procedures. The commutative and associative properties are comments on what is allowed and what is not as we seek to perform binary operations. They too are binary.

But in spite of our limited vocabulary, it is possible to consider adding or subtracting before we give any consideration to its implementation as the binary operation of addition or subtraction taking place over time. We can make statements about the total value of a group of numbers independently of the process of adding. That's what our shoppers do when they gauge their overflowing shopping carts and understand that the total cost is fully determined by the objects in the cart. We can understand the impact of a single number on the final value independently of the other numbers or variables in a sequence of additions and subtractions. That's what our shoppers do when they throw a $4.00 box of cereal in their cart. They understand that it increases by $4.00 the total cost of their purchases. This remains true even if the box of cereal is scanned first and is followed by scanning a $1.00 discount coupon justified by some other purchase. The resulting calculation, when the sequential constraint finally kicks in, is a subtraction: 4 − 1. The shoppers' perspective is better represented when we no longer look at 4 − 1 as a single unit, a subtraction, but consider instead each number on its own and its impact on the final value.

We used bubbles earlier to illustrate the shoppers' perspective and to help children assume it even with numbers unattached to things. The bubbles, of course, are just props used initially to help establish a certain vision, a vision that remains after the bubbles are discarded.

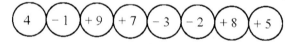

The vision facilitated by the use of bubbles associates each operation sign with the number that follows. Instead of a succession of operations (4 − 1 = 3; 3 + 9 = 12; 12 + 7 = 19, etc.), the eye focuses on a series of independent instructions to increase by 4 or by 9 or decrease by 1 or by 3. The mind considers the effect of each number and its operation sign on the final amount.

In contrast to the binary perspective of a succession of operations, this can be called the *unitary* perspective. The use of bubbles illustrates and facilitates a unitary perspective on a sequence of operations. It opens wide our imaginations to the flexibility of moving those bubbles around (or the operation sign and the number that follows once we no longer need the bubbles), while equipping us with the number sense that prevents us from adding 1 and 9 or 2 and 8 in the previous sequence.

> Somewhat to my surprise, I realized I was using bubbles with my students in a number of different circumstances. Each time, I now realize, it was an attempt to shift away from a binary perspective linking two numbers by an operation sign in order to focus on the unitary effect of each single sign-and-number combination.

For instance, we used bubbles earlier when attempting to engineer an approach to adding and subtracting integers that could speak to our students' intuition. The bubbles help us minimize the binary perspective of operations and strengthen a more intuitive perception of what each number contributes to the final value.

If we look at $-10 - 7$ as an operation, we encounter the clash between the sign for subtraction and the need to add. So we may be instructed to process the operation in terms of additive inverse, taking the difference between absolute values, and giving that difference the sign of the number with the larger absolute value. That's asking a lot of our students when our objective is to allow students to correctly evaluate the expression. Switching to the unitary perspective makes it possible instead to ignore real differences that no longer matter and see what the two numbers have in common. The perspective highlighted by the bubbles makes it clear that both numbers combine their efforts to push the finger down on the number line. This can be experienced and intuitively perceived as adding absolute values (the distances) and as resulting in a negative answer.

$-10 - 7$ Down and down: $(-10)(-7)$

We also used bubbles to highlight a unitary perspective when considering the important distributive property of multiplication over addition and subtraction.

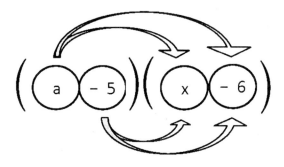

Here again, it is the sign-number combination seen in a unitary perspective that is distributed to each of the unitary terms within the second polynomial. In fact, the unitary perspective is used to break up the binary operations within parentheses.

The unitary perspective is prevalent in algebra as we focus more on variables and on individual terms than on operations. We group like terms when adding two polynomials, with no concern about the commutative and associative properties of addition. The unitary perspective prevails also when, on seeing $y = 3x - 5$, we choose to interpret it based on the standard model $y = mx + b$. We isolate $- 5$ in our minds and identify it as $b = -5$.

A similar analysis can be made of a series of multiplication and divisions where each number and the operation sign in front of it make their own specific contribution to the final answer. A "$\div 3$" anywhere in a sequence of multiplications and divisions has the effect of dividing the final answer by 3 compared to what it would otherwise be. A "$\times 10$" anywhere in the sequence multiplies the final answer by 10. As with additions and subtractions, each number and its associated operation can be freely moved around for our convenience. Any change that respects this unitary perspective is appropriate. Any grouping that doesn't, isn't.

For instance, let's compare $35 \times 12 \div 4 \div 7 \times 5$ to the same numbers and operation signs but with two sets of parentheses: $35 \times (12 \div 4) \div (7 \times 5)$. We want to know which of these grouping, if any, changes the value of the expression. Readers may want to answer the question themselves and watch the pathways of their own thinking as they do so.

The associative property of multiplication states that grouping two factors does not change the product. It applies to multiplication, not to division. I am not quite sure how it can help our students conclude that the grouping imposed by the first set of parentheses is acceptable while the second set changes the value of the expression. It may be easier to draw the correct conclusions by assuming the unitary perspective. With or without parentheses, "÷ 4" actually divides the final answer by 4 (with the parentheses, we multiply 35 by 3, which is equivalent to multiplying by 12 and dividing by 4). However, "× 5" multiplies by 5 as expected when used without parentheses but divides by 5 when the parentheses are added.

In fact, the unitary perspective represented by the bubbles fully illustrates why the commutative property applies to addition and multiplication, not to subtraction and division.

With 10 + 6, for instance, the binary perspective essentially looks at the operation. It allows the + sign for addition to remain unchanged in the middle while the two numbers switch position. So 10 + 6 = 6 + 10. Also with 10 × 6 = 6 × 10, the sign for multiplication remains unchanged between the two factors. This is what the commutative property describes. It is a perfectly valid perspective.

Instead of seeing the operation sign as between two numbers, the unitary perspective attaches the operation sign to the number that follows. In that perspective, with 10 − 6 or 10 ÷ 6, we cannot just keep the sign for the operation unchanged and switch the two numbers around. This would incorrectly transfer the implication of the signs for decreasing by 6 or dividing by 6 from the 6 to the 10. The commutative property does not apply to subtraction or division.

The freedom to move numbers around that we have recognized in our shoppers' perspective can also be achieved if we decide to eliminate subtraction as an operation and perform instead the same calculations as a series of additions of positive or negative numbers:

$$(+4) + (-1) + (+9) + (+7) + (-3) + (-2) + (+8) + (+5)$$

Now that we use only one operation, the sign for the operation loses its discriminatory power and much of its importance. The mind is free to focus on the integers. They associate sign and magnitude in ways that our bubbles emulate, allowing any one of the parentheses to switch position or combine with another.

Of course, asking students or shoppers to use the positive/negative approach to attain that flexibility would be the mathematical equivalent of Queen Marie Antoinette's response—"Let them eat cake"—to a population complaining of having no bread. There are significant number-sense benefits in helping students retain or acquire the unitary perspective right from the start.

As I allowed myself to look through the intuitive eyes of shoppers and students, the unitary perspective kept coming back in unexpected circumstances. I used bubbles to initially communicate the perspective to students. I didn't initially appreciate the significance of those bubbles or that they all had a common motivation. Giving the perspective a name and some theoretical justification may make it easier for educators and curriculum developers to include it in their pedagogical strategies and use it as a convenient substitute to cumbersome properties of operations.

9

Themes

In previous sections, we explored practical examples of teaching to intuition. Each in its own way included similar themes and concerns that illustrate what it means to teach to intuition. They offered different perspectives on the same fundamental concerns. Let's focus on some of these common themes.

1. Obvious

The obvious is an extreme form of the intuitive. And yet, like the intuitive, what is obvious to one person is not necessarily obvious to another. What is obvious to us depends on what we know. The obvious—and to an even greater extent the intuitive—needs to be revealed, discovered, taught, formulated, reviewed. I will begin with a few personal stories that, in some form or another, may help us focus on the nature and requirements of the obvious which we can then scale down and apply to the intuitive.

My concern with the obvious, it seems, goes back a long way. I must have been ten or eleven. It may seem strange nowadays, but we had dinner as a family. My two brothers and I took turns setting the table for the evening meal: knife and spoon on the right, fork on the left. I got it right some of the time, for which I can thank probability more than my own knowledge. Probability also made sure that I got it wrong most of the time. "Knife and spoon on the right, fork on the left," I was told repeatedly. "It's not difficult, is it? Why can't you get it right?" Well, I couldn't, until it occurred to me that when I have only one of these utensils in my hand, it's the spoon. It must be in my right hand. The fork, I know, is on the opposite side. With the fork in my left hand, the knife must be on the right. It makes sense. It's obvious. Now I know.

Can we imagine teaching some topics of math in the same way? Are there rules, procedures, and definitions that we repeat over and over, hoping that one day they will stick in our students' minds? Can we imagine turning things around so that a constant need to remind students just vanishes and a permanent source of frustration disappears? Even if the change is not so drastic, so easy, or so permanent, this is what takes place to some degree as a student seeking to calculate an area sets aside in a hundredth of a second a fleeting temptation to multiply two nonperpendicular distances or perceives adding two fractions with a common denominator as no different from adding dollars to dollars, fully bypassing the need for a memorized rule. This is what happens when we propose some connection or mental process to help students remember math facts or the distinction between two terms that students constantly confuse.

Quite a few years later, long before I thought of myself as a math teacher or went back to school to become one, I wrote a how-to book on financial calculators: *The HP 12C Made Easy*. In the introduction, I started with a dig at the owner's manual: "Teaching you how to build a

124

wall does not mean dumping a truckload of bricks on your front lawn." Then:

> The ideal is not so much to simplify as to make obvious. The obvious implies understanding the simplicity. As such, the most successful passages are those where the reader is left with the impression that he already knew it or at least that there is nothing that he needs to remember. If the reader cooperates in this approach, *if he strives to understand the simplicity rather than attempt to memorize the simple*, he will retain the creativity required to adjust to the infinite variety of circumstances encountered in the real world.

I couldn't have said it better now that I have become a math teacher. The Common Core Standards for Practice stress applying math to the real world. They understand, as I did then when I was teaching adult practitioners, that it is unrealistic to expect procedures devoid of understanding to help us make sense of the world we live in. That's what the Common Core State Standards mean when they state, "A lack of understanding effectively prevents a student from engaging in the mathematical practices."

During a seminar that went along with this manual, a student came up to me one day and asked me a question that took me by surprise. He asked, "Where did you learn all this?" It was a good question. With my PhD in literature, why was I teaching those MBAs, accountants, lawyers, and top professional investors about the time value of money? After a few seconds, I gave a sincere answer: "I just accepted the simplicity."

Here is another experience. I had volunteered to tutor university students in very basic math. That Saturday morning, maybe eight or nine students came to me for help. Two of them did not know that you can multiply a whole number by ten, a hundred, or a thousand by adding one, two, or three zeros. The first one welcomed the information: "Why didn't anybody tell me?" The answer is probably that, through high school, her teachers thought it was too obvious to mention. The other student had a different reaction. She almost panicked and said, "Don't confuse me! I know how to do it!" And she continued with a long multiplication ... which I think she got wrong because of some glitches in the alignment of columns. The new approach was threatening the fragile balancing act of memorized rules and procedures that represented math for that student. I should know better than to interfere with a juggler balancing half a dozen balls in the air at the same time.

Then there is this sixth grader. He was doing his homework, and I was supervising. He had a number of word problems, all on the same model. They implied finding the prime factors of two numbers, using those to find the greatest common factor (GCF), and essentially using that GCF as the answer to the word problem. He had already solved a few problems on the same model, and he read the next one aloud.

A teacher brings to school 148 pencils and 185 candies.

How many students are there in the classroom?

He immediately said, "Oh! That's easy! It's 37." I said, "Hey, why don't you do the work." He answered, "No, the difference is 37. It's a prime number. It has to be 37."

He was perfectly right. What was obvious to him had completely escaped me. I was impressed with the number of skills and concepts that had to be pulled together to come up with this answer in the blinking of an eye. I urged him to explain his answer on the homework sheet. He reacted with some anxiety, "No. I can't do that. I have to follow the model." And he did. In that class, for all math work, he had to conform to preordained procedures carefully mapped out in advance by the teacher. For him, it was like painting by the numbers. He just couldn't do it and, in the eyes of the teacher, was at best a D student. A lot of learning was taking place in the class but also a lot of unlearning.

Among other things, these experiences point out that what is obvious to someone is not necessarily obvious to others. The term *obvious* seems to imply that no teaching is required. But a fact is not of itself obvious or intuitive. Understanding has a lot to do with making something obvious. The obvious can be staring at us in the face, and yet we don't necessarily see it. We are misleading ourselves if we think of the "obvious" as a quality of the facts themselves or that as soon as a fact becomes obvious to us it is necessarily so for others. It is a quality given to a fact by the links, the perspective, and the understanding in our brain. It needs to be taught and acknowledged. It needs to be reviewed at every opportunity.

Planned activities and manipulatives can represent a major investment in time and often lead to the discovery of some form of pattern or understanding. They are an opportunity to make some mathematical truth obvious. But then, too often, we stop at the edge. Time does not allow for that extra push, the extra step that brings the obvious to a conscious recognition and for some lingering that allows the realization to sink in. There is no time left for formulations by students and exploitation through specific applications to mathematical facts and processes and to real-world circumstances. These can be missed opportunities. There is too great a confidence on the part of the teacher that the obvious and its implications are obvious to all.

At the same time, for students and teachers, when faced with an approach that brings out the obvious in some mathematical process, there is the danger of dismissing it with some version of "Well, that's obvious!" Because it is obvious, we fail to recognize that we were not aware of how obvious it was a few minutes earlier. It seems to us that some fleeting recognition of the truth at some earlier stage dispenses us from recognizing that by focusing on the obvious and giving the obvious its full weight, we are really facing a different reality. Instead of using the massively obvious nature of the fact as the core of our teaching strategy, we may revert to paying lip service to the understanding. I want to replace the dismissive "Well, that's obvious!" with a resounding "Wow! Now it's obvious!"

2. Connections

In teaching to intuition, we make conscious efforts to establish a multitude of connections of various kinds, on different levels, rather than allowing mathematical facts to remain in the brain as isolated truths. There is magic in establishing connections that go beyond the apparent importance of the connections themselves. Establishing even the simplest connection gives the brain a handle on the fact.

As we looked at fractions, we saw the meaning of "numerator" and "denominator," we linked the words with other words associated with "number" and "name." We used this to reinforce the understanding of 3/4 as "3 of something called a quarter." This strengthened our understanding that we can add quarters or tenths in the same way as we add books or students. But for some students, the connection with "number" and "name" may help them remember which of numerator or denominator is on top, which on the bottom. For others, the connection of "denominator" with "name" and "nominal" may work in the opposite direction than intended. Instead of "nominal" helping them understand the connection between "name" and "denominator," their new understanding of "denominator" may help them understand a new word: "nominal." As teachers, we are satisfied with building connections. The hope and expectation is that they will be used in ways that stretch beyond our limited perspectives.

A teacher realizes that some students find it difficult to remember which is which of *complementary* and *supplementary* angles, which is associated with right angles, which with straight lines. No amount of repetition is likely to solve the teacher's pedagogical challenge. We need to find a connection, any connection. Where do we find right angles? Don't tell students, ask them. Let students look around and tell you. With very little prodding, the class may conclude that we find right angles in corners; that's where they hide. *C*orners and *C*omplementary share the same initial letters, as do *s*upplementary and *s*traight angle. We've established a connection that may permanently help students remember. We've taught our students two things: an approach to remembering which is which of those pairs of angles and a strategy that they can apply in other circumstances where they find it difficult to remember.

Crucial to knowing multiplication facts is the link with sound and rhythm that can be created in the early grades. But other links can also be found to help students remember those facts. When connections are established with the right patterns, the 9 times multiplication facts become some of the easiest to master. The ability to immediately divide even digits by 2, the ability to see 24 in 48 and 21 in 42, creates links that tie facts together, helping 3×7 come to the rescue of 6×7.

That same ability to connect some numbers with their halves or doubles also provides a mental strategy for multiplying by 5. To multiply by 5, I can divide by 2 and multiply by 10, or vice versa. What is 5×28? It is 140. What is 5×24? It is 120. What is 5×8? It is 40. Consciously practiced with larger numbers, the connection remains as a background perception with the smaller numbers we want to include in essential multiplication facts. We want students to immediately know 5 × 8, but some awareness of the connection between 8 and the 4 of 40 or 6 and the 3 of 30 also contributes to the knowledge. These connections can be used as learning strategies. Establishing a wide network of connections around math facts could lighten the weight of endless and often hopeless efforts to memorize that contribute early in their studies at convincing children that they are not good at math.

I have made it clear that I am not a great friend of artificial mnemonic devices. But let me recognize that they create a link and that any link is better than no connections at all. Along with the Common Core State Standards, I objected earlier to the use of the mnemonic FOIL. I did so only because the mnemonic substitutes itself to a greater number of more productive connections. If there were no better alternatives, no logical pattern in the procedure, FOIL would establish a welcome connection that could help students multiply binomials.

A roman author gave as advice to would-be writers to let no day go by without writing a line: "No day without a line!" We could use as a motto: "No fact without a connection!"

Patterns and structures are an essential form of connection. They are not necessarily a mathematical absolute. We established a connection between all the formulas for area and volume that our students are likely to encounter. Each formula is no longer the isolated statement it would otherwise be. The connection is not a mathematical absolute, and as such, we may be reluctant to use it. Or we may feel compelled to attach a footnote each time we refer to it, noting the exception. Our duty is to what happens in the brains of our students, not to some theoretical mathematical accuracy that can take care of itself when the time is right. I am happy with letting children contrast squares and rectangles for a few years before they broaden their understanding to seeing squares as a particular kind of rectangle.

Our overview of the structure of the four operations is replete with connections. For instance, noticing that multiplication, when seen in context, has two very different kinds of factors leads directly to an understanding that there are two kinds of divisions. Our understanding that we can only add and subtract things that have the same name allows us to contrast those two forms of divisions in word problems: we have the repeat subtraction version of division only when the two number words in the problem are the same. The observation makes it easier for students to recognize situations in the real world that can be analyzed with that version of division.

Understanding is the quintessential connection. It establishes a connection between patterns and understandings we already have in our minds and the new material we want to teach. The recognition that occurs is a connection taking place.

The Common Core Standards for Practice urge modeling the outside world with the tools of mathematics, helping us analyze that world and make sense of it in mathematical terms. That too is establishing connections between the mathematics that we know and the world we live in. In *Teaching to Intuition*, on many instances, we have strengthened that connection by allowing our understanding of the real world to enlighten us on the processes of mathematics.

Sometimes, when I suggest a connection that may help some students understand or remember, colleagues tell me, "Oh, I use that other approach." I don't see connections as necessarily exclusive of one another. Not only are students able to choose those that make more sense to them, but many can coexist in a single mind. I see knowledge as existing at the crossroads of a web of connections, some crucial, some trivial, a few even purely artificial. Even My Dear Aunt Sally might find some indulgence on my part if she didn't insist on being the only queen of the party.

On a variety of levels, we can see teaching to intuition as consciously nurturing networks of connections in our students' minds. Connections help students remember, and that is important. But beyond helping memory, connections are the essence of understanding, modeling, imagination, and creativity. By showing the consistency of mathematics, they are a key to seeing the beauty of mathematical thought and practice.

3. The Brain

As teachers, our concern with the brain is constant and omnipresent. What picture do we have of our students' brains? Let's choose between the two images shown here and ask ourselves which one we are addressing as we speak to our students.

 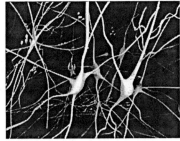

The first picture, with its neat shelves, illustrates our very worthwhile attempt at making things clear to students. But it is not the real brain. The real brain is much more complex, powerful, creative, diverse, and messy. We have an obligation to help students organize and classify the facts of mathematics and make it as easy as we can for students to grasp and remember. But if our picture of the brain is limited to those neat little shelves where facts can be stored in correct order and retrieved by columns and rows, we are deceiving ourselves and shortchanging our students.

The brain is made up of billions of interconnected neurons. Information is stored as networks of connections. New connections are created as we acquire new knowledge and are synonymous with that acquisition. As we learn, the brain grows. It establishes new neural pathways. That's what learning is. Teachers and students can consciously cooperate in that growing process. Students need to understand that they are not just learning new facts; they are growing their brains and their intelligence in the process. The qualities of rigor, logic, balance, and symmetry; the seeking out and discovery of patterns; the objectivity of the mathematical pursuit; the perseverance in the quest for answers; the steady accretion of more far-reaching conclusions; all this and other features of mathematics get imprinted into the brain and set patterns of connections that have consequences in life beyond their mathematical models.

We encourage that growth as we see facts and present facts to students, not just as isolated truths but as part of a growing web of connections.

The connections that we create may be simplistic in terms of what the brain itself develops. But they set the tone. They create the veins and arteries and leave the network of capillaries to the creative processes of the brain itself. I like to constantly remind students of the two levels. I like students to be aware of the conscious connections that learning establishes and of the hidden powerhouses of their brains that work faster, better, more creatively than all conscious connections.

An example of this can be found in geometry, when students are taught about proofs. I tell students that the careful sequencing of mathematical truths—definitions, axioms, and theorems—that we think of as a proof in geometry, and in particular the marvelous sequencing of reasons that makes up Euclidean geometry, is not how we find the solution to a geometric problem: it's how we explain the solution to others. As we look for the solution, our minds are much faster, more creative, and messier than allowed by a neat sequence of theorems. They shoot inquiries in all directions, inspired by knowledge of facts, experience of patterns, analogies with previous quests for answers. The inquiries are initiated, tested, rejected, or retained much faster than possible if each step had to be given a name and was formally considered.

And suddenly, things seem to fit together. We think we have our solution. As we look for the shortest road to justify our conclusion, as we formulate connections and carefully string theorems, we hope to end up with a formal proof. We may also realize that we didn't quite get it right and may have to start over again with the messy exploration but with a heightened insight and a better chance of getting it right this time around. Many geometry students find this understanding of the process extremely liberating. It sets them free to cast a wide, creative web of inquiry. They no longer feel constrained to a cautious step-by-step procedure in the initial stages of problem solving.

In our quest to leave no child behind, there may be a tendency to teach to the neat shelves of our first illustration instead of to the real brain. We may break down processes into simple steps that we number; we may ask students to list those steps as they explain their thinking. But is it then really their thinking? Or are we imposing a uniformity that is essentially the opposite of thinking? When we ask students to show their work are we preventing some from using mental math? As we ask them to give their reasons, are we limiting them to the steps we have demonstrated and the reasons we have given? I too want to give clear explanations; I too want students who can explain their thinking to others. But there is danger in requiring the two explanations, mine and the student's, to be the same.

An answer to what is a real dilemma, to the delicate balancing act that is pedagogy, may be first in teachers who are very much aware of the danger. Instead of aiming for students who will all echo our reasons and even our formulations, perhaps we could often challenge the class to provide as many different explanations as possible or at least an alternative one, an alternative formulation. These will not all be as good as ours, as complete, as well formulated, but they may show a path to understanding that we had not thought of. The benefit will not be only in validating students who suggest alternatives but in encouraging the teacher to resist the very natural tendency to favor some exclusive official explanation.

Recognizing and perhaps highlighting for the class the sliver of truth we discover in sometimes clumsy or incomplete explanations offered by students may demand imagination on the part of the teacher and some indulgence as we are talking of concepts and modes of thinking that students find difficult to put into words. "What is an umbrella?" we ask a student. We expect a description of the contraption. The student answers: "An umbrella is, when it rains, we open it up to keep dry." The child knows what an umbrella is. We can acknowledge that knowledge before we probe for more details or seek an answer from another student.

Let's imagine asking students who have just correctly added 2/7 and 3/7 to explain what they have just done. "I add the numerators and keep the common denominator" has to be a valid answer. But what about "2 + 3 = 5"? In some ways, it is less satisfying than the previous explanation, as it makes no references to the denominator, and it could be rejected as too simplistic. In other ways, it may demonstrate more understanding than the first answer which could be just parroting a meaningless process. If students are asked to add 2 apples and 3 apples and justify the answer, we would be satisfied with "2 + 3 = 5." We would not need to be told that 5 represents 5 apples, not 5 oranges. It's too obvious to mention. Maybe the second answer shows a student who has really internalized the understanding that there is no difference between adding sevenths and adding apples, a student who adds correctly without having to eliminate incorrect alternatives such as a 5 that would mysteriously change into 5 of a different denominator any more than two groups of apples would suddenly turn into oranges when added.

To justify the process used to find an equivalent fraction, students may state some version of "I multiplied by 1" or "Each part is smaller, but I have more parts." These are two very different explanations, essentially different paths to the same procedure. They are both correct. They are also not exclusive of one another, even in the same brain. But a student could also answer in very practical terms, "I eat as much pizza if I eat one half or two quarters." We may then ask for different formulations, but a well-meaning requirement for a more specific explanation, one instantly couched in mathematical terms, could lead to a vision of mathematics as a single simplistic path to math understanding, one where set explanations become the new procedures mechanically enforced and easy to test. Students have a right to be on a different wave-length than the teacher. Thinking does not tolerate being put in a straitjacket.

Mathematics cannot be limited to a single neurological pathway flashing through the brain, the same for all on any given topic. There is mathematical life one level below conscious logic and deliberate procedure. The better activities seek to develop students' ability to tap that dimension of the power of their brains, as do the better interactions between teacher and students. The connections created are more subtle than what could immediately be put into words. Thinking is a messy process and will not be the same for all. Maybe our intimate acquiescence with mathematical truths has its roots at that deeper level. It is at that less conscious level that students can manifest their individuality, their preferred approaches to learning and understanding.

4. Metacognition

Concern with the workings of the brain and of the learning process is not restricted to teachers. We want students to become aware of what takes place in their minds. We don't just ask them to know and understand, but we ask for their cooperation in the process of expanding their brains to new knowledge and new understanding.

At every turn, we find students who do not use their brains. There are some who, when faced with a math question, have been trained to think that they don't know the math if they can't immediately blurt out the answer. When we encounter that attitude, we need to challenge the student not just on the specific topic but on the approach to knowing math and doing math that it implies. We don't even need to be very subtle. "When I asked you that question, did you take time to think things out? Why not? Do you think that I have an immediate answer to all the math questions I am asked? For you, is math something that you know or don't know, or is it a thinking activity? Is it all right for you to answer, 'I don't know. I'd like to think about it'? Do you want to tell me that right now?" Or to a whole class, "Okay, class. I'm going to ask you a question. I don't want any hands to go up until I tell you. I want you to take time to think." Students need to be told and taught that mathematics is a thinking activity.

In discussing with students their answers to the 'three important questions', we helped them discover what they already knew about adding things that have a different name. We helped them look into the working of their own brains to transfer that intuitive knowledge to the need for a common denominator when adding fractions. We encouraged students to listen to what their brains were telling them, just as you can listen to your body or ignore its pains and urgings. We encouraged students to interpret confusion as their brains talking to them. "What is it trying to tell you?" Instead of submitting to confusion, of being frustrated by it and using it as an excuse for allowing their brains to shut down, it can be taken as a positive encouragement to inquire into the cause of the confusion. Students need to learn that in problem solving, they are often closest to a solution when they are faced with an apparent contradiction. They have the solution cornered. It lies in the only option that resolves the contradiction. We want to train students to overcome the panic of not knowing and accept it as a first step in the knowing process.

Helping students become aware of what they already know, of the workings of their own brains, of their patterns of thought, is an important part of teaching to intuition. It means helping students discover that math is not just a collection of facts that they have to memorize but a process that exists inside their brains. Math is not in the textbook; it is not in the homework and exercises that they do. It is inside their brains not just as a collection of truths but as acquiescence to those truths and as an engaged, creative, living process.

In practice, as a first step, it may mean just telling students, "It's not what you write down on paper that matters, it's what remains in your brain." And we back up that statement by not giving them busywork, by choosing quality over quantity, by respecting their own brains' approach to learning and to solving problems, by fostering and welcoming creative solutions, by giving them enough time to make mistakes and learn from those mistakes, by helping them focus on what there is inside those brains of theirs, and by shifting the grading more generously to what has been learned than to what has been turned in. After all, *it's not what they write down on paper that matters, it's what remains in their brains.*

In asking them to learn math, we are encouraging them to consciously and formally cooperate in the process of growing their brains.

LESS INTUITIVE	MORE INTUITIVE
Memorized	Understood
Imposed	Discovered Guided discovery Agree with the truth
Procedural, recipe	Obvious
Isolated fact Single explanation	Multiple connections Part of pattern, structure
One-dimensional	Knowledge existing as a network of connections
Abstract	Concrete
General	Specific
Word-dependent	Experienced, familiar Practical, applied, useful Visual, sensory, art, rhythm
Expecting immediate response Tendency to blurt out answer	Time to think it out, to make and correct errors Patient sense-making

LESS INTUITIVE	**MORE INTUITIVE**
Learned in isolation	Collaborative discovery Shared with others Explained to others
Drilled	Practiced Applied Knowledge found in the deeper reaches of the mind
Doubt Confusion Uncertainty	Confidence Ownership Alternative ways of verifying, checking truth
Passive acceptance	Active learning Creative, questioning attitude
Suffered and rejected	Enjoyed Challenging Life-long learner
Stuff the brain	Grow your brain

Add your own contrasting approaches towards learning, teaching, knowing.

10

Strategies

As we seek to teach to intuition, we use a number of very simple strategies. I am including here a sampling. Some are essentially reserved for the teacher. Others are used and modeled by the teacher and students can learn to use them as thinking and problem-solving strategies.

1. The Five-Second Review

It would be great if students remembered forever what we have explained once. But that's not the way it is. That's where the five-second review comes in. It consists in missing no opportunity to refer back to a concept or an understanding as we go through routine mathematical interactions with our students. In our attempt to make mathematics more intuitive and less reliant on memorized rules and procedures, the five-second review, though very simple, is one of our most powerful tools. It embodies the essence of what it means to teach to intuition: the transfer of a reliance on formulations that all too often take over from understanding to a willingness to trust the understanding as the major permanent source of the knowledge.

Explanations and understanding are routinely used when a topic is initially introduced. They are then summarized into a rule or procedure. The tendency is to rely on rule and procedure from then on, with the understanding allowed to fade away over time. A five-second-review comment aims to prevent that from happening. It seeks to embed the understanding as the central source of the knowledge over the long run by throwing out a hint of the inner logic, revealing connections or intuitive perspectives. It allows us to review concept and understanding as often as it is customary to review rules. The five-second review can be as simple as a gesture, the order we write things on the board, a casual comment, or a question that *refers back to something that has been seen in more detail* earlier and that clearly brings out *the more intuitive perspective on the process.* It really takes no time at all, as it is at most a running comment on an action that is taking place anyway. Once we have decided to teach to intuition, it is almost just thinking aloud.

We have many opportunities to use the five-second review during any math period, at all grade levels, on just about any topic, without any fear of being repetitive any more than we are repetitive when we refer back to a rule. It has its purpose even if we think it is no longer needed, as it confirms, beyond the topic at hand, the fundamental attitude we want to adopt toward what it means to know math. Despite our best efforts, students will have constant opportunities—through other teachers, tutors, parents, fellow students, test material, and textbooks—to revert to procedures and rules instead of intuition. For most, knowledge will consist of a blend between knowing the rule and the understanding, in different proportions for each student, in different proportions over time for any one student. We too will often summarize the understanding with a description that could become the rule. But we want to use every opportunity to remind students of the alternative approach and to give them every possible chance to avoid a practice of math as a mindless interaction of memorized rules and procedures.

Examples of the five-second review are scattered throughout the topics discussed in *Teaching to Intuition*. Here are some examples.

In an initial section, we use strategies to bring adding and subtracting fractions within the scope of intuition, as opposed to relying exclusively on memorized rules. We then resort to five-second-review strategies to remind students of that understanding and even of the experience. For instance, if a student faced with adding 2/9 and 5/9 wants to add both numerators and denominators, we might ask, "What's 2 books and 5 books?" To add 2/7 and 3/5, instead of reminding a student of the need for a common denominator, we could say, "Can you add 2 cats and 3 dogs?" or "What's 2 sons and 3 daughters?" Or we might want to ask a simpler question, "What's 2/7 and 3/7?" If the student responds by saying, "5/7, of course!" we may already have reminded him of the contrast between the ease of adding when we have a common denominator and the impossibility of doing so until we do. The teacher will gauge what works, what doesn't work, maybe what needs to be reviewed more thoroughly. The five-second review finds its justification in our conviction that knowledge resides in the understanding, not essentially in the formulation that might tend to replace the understanding, and in the realization that understanding and concepts need to be practiced as often as rules and procedures.

We discussed earlier an approach to teaching addition and subtraction of integers that has the ambition of making the need to teach the topic in community college remedial classes a thing of the past. If this can be achieved, it represents a significant saving of time and dollars and an opportunity for many to begin acquiring a new confidence in their mathematical abilities. Yet, the five-second-review comments that refresh a student's understanding may be as simple as asking, "Do you need all those + signs?" or pointing to a mark on the table and saying, "This is zero. Show me with your finger!" or "Are you going more up than down?" or "Think of it as a temperature change!" or "Do you like it when the umpire cancels a 5-yard penalty on your team?" Having calculated $-10 - 7 = -17$, we may comment, "As you see, -17 is 7 units smaller than -10," a short reminder of the way it is with negative numbers. They are brief reminders of an experience or an understanding that substitute to a constant repetition of a rule.

We mentioned using the order in which we write things on the board as examples of five-second-review strategies. As an example, let's imagine we have just concluded that we need 56 as the common denominator for adding 3/7 and 5/8. I can rush ahead and implement the decision, or by my actions and running commentary, I may choose to model the reasoning that a student might follow and review some of the major characteristics of fractions.

148

So I want an equivalent fraction with 56 as its denominator.

How do I change 7 into 56? That's easy! I multiply 7 by 8.

In the process, I've made the fraction 8 times smaller than it should be, 3/56 instead of 3/7. So let me multiply the numerator by 8. I get 24/56. Now each part is 8 times smaller, but I have 8 times more parts: the value has not changed.

I need to do the same with 5/8. How can I change 8 into 56?

We may then choose to point out that we have multiplied by 1, showing a different perspective on the same process.

As teachers, we cannot both lament in the teachers' room or in a presidential commission how important it is for students to master operations on fractions and how poorly many perform on the topic—and then dismiss as inconsequential the opportunities we have of reviewing the basic structure of fractions. Here, the order we choose and our running commentary provide a review of some essential understanding in hardly more time than it takes to perform the transformation.

On other topics that we have examined, five-second-review opportunities may be as simple as systematically asking students to identify which model of division is used when solving a division word problem or modeling a right angle with an open hand on the palm of the other hand when students are finding the area of geometric figures. Just about every simple addition or subtraction calculation can be an opportunity to help students visualize the operation on a vertical number line. We may hint at a convenient benchmark which transforms the addition or subtraction process from a pure manipulation of numbers to the reminder of an experience with the finger on the number line and a mental strategy. What is 57 − 14? A five-second-review prompt may ask, "From 57, how far down do you go to reach 50? ... How much further do you need to go to subtract 14?" If a student does not remember 6 × 7, we can ask, "What's 3 × 7? ... Can you double 21?" We are reminding the student of a mental strategy and reviewing connections between facts. A student at the board has successfully multiplied 27 × 52. We are not satisfied with the practice of a procedure. We initiate a mental check on the magnitude of the answer: "What's 3 × 5? What's 30 × 50? Does your answer make sense?" We have in the process reviewed rounding and multiplying by multiples of 10. We have reignited in the student an understanding that math is an activity of the mind, one that doesn't blindly surrender to the result given by a procedure.

On any one of these topics, those mental strategies are not taught by a single presentation on the topic. They deserve as much practice as procedures normally get. They become a habit of mind through repeated exposure and modeling over time. That's where a five-second-review habit on the part of the teacher comes in.

2. Progression

Progression establishes a special kind of connection. As we use it here, it transfers understanding from the familiar to what is less so. We all practice it as we guide students over time through various stages of sophistication on just about any topic. We use it as we preface an explanation with a quick review of prerequisites. But it can also be used on the micro level, as a habit of mind that consists in taking a step back to more familiar material or simpler numbers as an introduction to the more complex situation that is our real interest at that time. It can be used by the teacher as a teaching strategy or by the student as a problem-solving strategy. Progression can help us transfer to the less familiar the understanding that we have of a fact or process under simpler circumstances.

I like to think that difficulties do not just add up: they multiply. A level 7 difficulty combined with one that could be rated as a 3 can represent a level 21 difficulty for our students. Progression is an effort to minimize that effect by helping students, for instance, focus on the level 3 difficulty before combining it with the level 7.

We suggested earlier that students could use the repeat subtraction model of division as a way of making sense of division by a fraction. Our interest was to remind students that $3/5 \div 1/5$ answers the question, "How many times does $1/5$ go in to $3/5$?" But any sensitivity to what goes on in a student's mind makes it clear that such a statement may not immediately make sense for all students, even if previous explanations and practice

151

mean that it should. So we can first submit a simpler problem such as 15 ÷ 5 = 3, stating that this calculation answers the question, "How many times does 5 go into 15?" Because the numbers are familiar and the answer is so obvious, students easily give their full acquiescence to the statement. They can then transfer the statement and the understanding to dividing the fractions. The initial step back to simpler whole numbers has only postponed the focus on fractions by a few seconds, but we are much more likely to have all the students understand when we formulate the meaning of division in terms of fractions.

We can use the approach on a number of topics almost as five-second-review statements on understanding and concepts.

When calculating the area of triangles, for instance, a first example can be a right triangle where the two legs are the height and the base and the hypotenuse is the diagonal of a rectangle, clearly identifying the area of the triangle as 1/2 of that of the rectangle. Students have been reminded not of a formula but of the reason. In work sheets or practice material, we may make a point of selecting our first examples as reminders of the concept or thought process we want our students to practice, or we may want to draw attention to the difficulty they may face.

When modeling practical situations, the difference between adding and subtracting is sharp and obvious: we know which one we want to perform. In a work sheet on adding and subtracting fractions, the choice between adding and subtracting is purely circumstantial and easy for students to ignore as they focus their attention on the procedure. A student who mistakenly adds correctly when the two fractions should be subtracted gets the answer wrong more through inattention than through ignorance. What about a gentle reminder to pay attention to the operation sign by having on occasion or as the first example the two same fractions to add and then subtract? Similarly, we may give a hint not to add denominators by having as our first example 2/769 + 3/769 instead of the usual one- or two-digit denominators that can be added without paying attention to what is being done. Our motivation as teachers for doing so is our concern for the weaker, more easily distracted students in our class. We base our teaching strategies not on what students are supposed to know or do but on what can help those weaker students focus on what we really want them to practice. We constantly remind ourselves that any example or practice is not meant to be just a test but a teaching tool, even a constant reteaching tool. We want to leave no child behind.

Progression: The Six-Two Strategy

Word problems or number stories represent an essential form of mathematical modeling, one encouraged by the Common Core Standards for Practice. Let's take an example, analyze some of the difficulties students may encounter, and suggest some way of using progression from simple to more complex as a strategy for solving the problem and mastering the concept.

> A hurricane is predicted. All 17,931 inhabitants
> of Baton Bleu need to be evacuated by bus. Each
> bus can hold 43 passengers.
> How many buses—or rather bus trips—do we
> need?

Here, we have a word problem on the simplest level.
Yet, number stories of this kind often remain a challenge
even for pre-algebra students. We have to decide, how
do we teach something so fundamental that it should
rely more on a student's intuitive understanding of the
meaning of division than on any teachable procedure?

As with most word problems, a first difficulty lies in the
fact that it is a make-believe situation, one not directly
experienced by the students. Without understanding the
narrative, there is no solution. We cannot expect
students to solve a word problem unless they can tell the
story themselves in their own words. As I read the word
problem, I do not pay much attention to the details of the
numbers. I'll do that when I am ready to punch them
into the calculator or write them down as a long
division. Disregarding the number is not a skill mastered
by most students. The first number is not easy to read.
We may see students stumble as they do so. In other
words, so much of their attention may be taken up by
confronting and taking in 17,931 down to the last unit
that their minds may find it difficult to grasp the
indispensable story line.

I was driving back from school on the freeway, just
where the 118 blends into the 210 East, frustrated at
how much difficulty my remedial ninth graders were
having with such problems and how convoluted and

artificial were the strategies offered by the textbook to help them make the choice. Then it hit me: six two. Those problems would be significantly easier if we replaced the larger number with 6 and the smaller one with 2. Let's replace the previous problem with this one:

> 6 students need to be driven to the game.
> Each car can only carry 2 students.
> How many cars do we need?

Now the *immediacy* of the arithmetic helps students focus on what we are really interested in: honing our students' intuitive perception of which operation to use. Students may give the correct answer, 3 cars, even before they formally identify which operation they performed to reach that solution. Their intuition took over. They can then conclude that a division is what allowed them to reach 3 from their knowledge of 6 and 2. The experience can help them properly interpret an identical or similar problem that uses larger, more confusing numbers.

So we have a strategy that can be applied in a number of ways. We can initially provide extensive practice with simple word problems that use only these two numbers. With no numbers to remember except 6 and 2, it becomes easy for students to tell the story in their own words. The simple numbers and intuitive answer helps them become familiar with the structure of these word problems and the operation that solves them. We can later teach students to identify the larger and the smaller numbers in a number story and, as they read the problem aloud or repeat them in their own words, to substitute 6 for the larger and 2 for the smaller number. Having solved the problem under those conditions, they can then transfer that understanding to the original numbers. We are allowing them to practice the essential discrimination skills needed to choose between the different operations. We are also teaching them to somewhat disregard the specifics of the numbers as they focus on the story line and the relationship between those numbers. Just as progression can help students transfer understanding from whole numbers to fractions, so at an earlier stage, it can help transfer understanding from simple numbers to larger, more intimidating ones.

We cannot ask students to choose easier numbers on their own. Most other numbers would not have the same impact. So we make the choice for them: 6 and 2. The number 6 is divisible by 2. These are the two smallest numbers where all four operations yield different whole-number answers: 3, 4, 8, and 12. Students can become particularly familiar using the four operations with word problems that use these two numbers.

I'm a little bit concerned that you didn't pay enough attention to what I was saying. Let me check. What freeway was I on when I came up with the strategy, or did you pay no attention to the numbers?

3. Flexibility

Flexibility, as we use it here, is our minds' ability to switch from one mathematical interpretation to another, perhaps only for a few seconds, just because we feel like it or because it helps us better understand what is going on. The flexibility principle encourages us to recognize different ways of thinking about the same mathematical idea or practice. Common Core Standard for Mathematical Practice No. 7 refers to flexibility as students are expected to see structures from different perspectives: "[Students] also can step back for an overview and shift perspective. They can see complicated things, such as some algebraic expressions, as single objects or as being composed of several objects." Teachers can encourage students to use flexibility to help their mathematical thinking; they can encourage that flexibility as a general characteristic of their thinking processes.

At the heart of flexibility, there is an understanding that math is just that: math. It's just a tool that can be applied to a great variety of situations. There is also marvel at the immense variety of circumstances that real life offers—or that our busy minds imagine—to which math can apply. Nothing is quite as simple or as one sided as we may wish. So the tool of mathematics finds itself pressed into service in strange ways. Different ways of looking at a mathematical object or a mathematical procedure are not contradictory. One does not exclude the others. Teachers need to communicate to students that very different interpretations are compatible, almost accomplices.

The language of mathematics reflects circumstances and applications that may no longer be the only ones possible. It retains fossilized remains of its earlier limitations. I have the right, the flexibility, to take a mathematical tool designed for a particular purpose and to use it for another purpose. I have the right to do so without necessarily being constrained by the vocabulary to limit my applications to circumstances that fit into the mold of that vocabulary. Math is blind to what I do with it. Too strict an interpretation of the original meaning of some mathematical terms can stifle our quest for creative flexibility.

As a prime example, let's take the words "whole number" and "fraction." The vocabulary reflects an original contrast between the two. Some numbers are whole. Others are not whole. They are what we get when we break up the whole into pieces; they are fractions of the whole. They are fractions.

But fractions are a beautiful tool. I am free to use that tool to perform mathematical magic on more than the whole—and we have "improper fractions." I am even free to decide to change a whole number into a fraction, just by giving it a denominator of 1. I can then apply to 5 or 19, for example, written as 5/1 and 19/1, procedures that have been developed primarily for more authentic fractions.

> We listed earlier different ways of thinking about a fraction such as 3/4. Generally, because of the circumstances, one interpretation makes more sense than the other. But math does not know the difference between all these interpretations. The fraction 3/4 is all of them at the same time. I know the difference, but math does not. That is the power of math. It is consistent and objective. Things turn out all right whatever interpretation I decide to give to 3/4. And that is also the power of my brain: for a

> fraction of a second, I may decide for my convenience to change my perspective, to apply to "3/4 the number" characteristics or procedures that are normally associated with "3/4 the division" or "3/4 the proportion."

Flexibility allows me to see squares and rectangles in contrast to one another, to sort them out as such, and also to see squares as a special kind of rectangle. When needed, the formal definition will be given full respect, but I don't need to allow it to constrain my thinking when the contrast is more important than their common features. I know few teachers who, if they asked students to draw a square, a rectangle, and a parallelogram, would give full credit to a student who had drawn only a square, even though the child might make the point that it stands for all three figures and ask the teacher, "Which one did I forget?"

We saw two possible ways of looking at a series of operations, the binary perspective that focuses on operations and the unitary that focuses on each number and its operation sign. Flexibility allows us to choose the perspective that helps us most in a given circumstance. Flexibility also allows me to think of 372×941 as a multiplication or as a single number in factored form. In a right triangle, it allows me to think of a side that measures 5 inches as the unit side, which allows me to identify the other sides in terms of trigonometric functions. For a fraction of a second, I use my own personal unit. A more frequent switch in units identifies 12 inches as 1 foot. But units are arbitrary, and I am free to invent my own.

It is objectively difficult, as we hold one perspective in mind, to understand that others who may hold different perspectives do not immediately understand what seems so clear to us. Similarly, we may find it difficult to follow the argument of a student who is looking at a situation from a different but equally valid perspective from ours.

There is math. It has been created, honed, expanded. And there's me and my creative mind, living in this big, diverse world of ours. These are two different layers. Math is not the dictator of how I use math. It is my servant, and within reasonable constraints of truth, logic, and consistency, it bends to my will, my needs, my convenience, and my creativity. Students can learn the power that they have over mathematics and contrast it to a sense of subservience and powerlessness that is often theirs in relation to math.

4. Lazymath

Lazymath, as I use it, consists in accomplishing some mathematical task in some kind of nontraditional and simpler way. It is not normally applicable to all instances of that activity, otherwise it would be chosen as the traditional way of achieving that result.

We used lazymath earlier with operations on fractions when we focused on operations that can be performed using no other rule than those used to add, subtract, multiply, and divide books or apples.

If I ask students, "Is there a lazymath option?" they will know that they should look for a more creative alternative than the usual approach, such as a simple mental math strategy. It is one form of flexibility. When finding the area of a triangle, if base or height are even, students can be urged by the question to divide that even number by 2 instead of multiplying b × h before dividing. How often do we see a student multiply two or more factors when the next step consists in finding the prime factors of the product? The lazymath approach consists in going directly from the factors to the prime factors without ever bothering to know what the product would be.

Lazymath draws students' attention not to a meaningless shortcut but to the availability of a nontraditional, generally simpler approach. Its use helps students break the tendency to rely blindly on procedures or routine approaches. It helps students develop useful mental math skills and can often help them focus on concepts.

5. Two Wrongs Make a Right

In life outside of mathematics, we sometimes say, "Two wrongs don't make a right." By this, we mean that if your neighbor refuses to do anything about his dog barking all night, it doesn't give you the right to throw an old shoe through his window. Here, we say the opposite. We will use the expression to link in our students' minds a great variety of instances based on the same two-step pattern.

Here are some examples.

"To divide by a fraction, you multiply ..." The sentence is incomplete, but if we stopped here, it would be an absurdity. Division and multiplication are two different operations. You can't just replace division by multiplication and get away with it. So the rest of the sentence corrects the initial error: "by the reciprocal." That also, on its own, would be an absurdity. You can't just replace a number by its reciprocal. But in this instance, and in many others, the second "mistake" corrects the first one.

"To subtract an integer, add ... its opposite." Many mathematical processes are implementations of the "two wrongs make a right" principle. The principle is an essential process of mental math where, to multiply 49 by 6, we multiply 50 by 6 ... and subtract 6; to add 37 and 99, we add 100 ... and correct our "error" by subtracting 1.

So even as students refer back to the rule for some of these procedures, we want them to recognize a pattern that they will find in a great variety of very different circumstances. It gives some logical consistency to the rule. It makes it more difficult for students to make just one change and expect things to remain the same. It trains students to expect the other shoe to drop. It creates one more thread in the web of connections that becomes part of their thinking patterns.

"Two wrongs make a right" is the expression that we can use and that students can use to identify the pattern as it is recognized. It is just one example of a constant attempt on the part of teachers to look beyond the immediate procedure at a wider context, at a pattern that can be recognized elsewhere, and in the process to build a rich and creative mathematical experience.

6. Expectations

To divide by 10, 100, or 1000, we move the decimal point 1, 2, or 3 places to the left ... or is it to the right?

However, we don't need to know.

To divide by 10, 100, or 1000, we move the decimal point 1, 2, or 3 spaces ... in whatever direction makes the number 10, 100, 1000 times smaller.

Our expectation about the relative magnitude of the answer is all we need to know. In fact, our expectation is all we should know. The more mathematically minded students will do so on their own. For others, even formulating the rule in terms of left or right confirms them in a tendency to feel insecure and at a loss if they have not memorized a procedure. Instead, we should want to build confidence in their ability to think. Let's think about it: Left? Right? Do we really want to entrust the knowledge to our students' ability to remember if it's left or right? Will my students be left helpless if temporarily or permanently they forget? What a short shelf life compared to understanding.

The problem with not formulating the rule in terms of left or right is precisely that: we don't know how to formulate the rule any other way. But that is our problem, not the students' problem. I would like to say, it's our hang-up. We feel compelled to formulate a rule, even if the rule is useless and counterproductive. I want to actively focus on welcoming the understanding, the simplicity, the obvious nature of the facts, not the empty wording I may be tempted to substitute for them.

So left or right? I don't know. I don't want my students to know. Instead of asking students to remember, teaching to their understanding will ask them to rely on their expectations.

Asking them for their expectations concerning an answer teaches students a crucial habit of mind, one that can be almost constantly actively engaged. What else does it mean to think if it doesn't include thinking ahead? The Common Core State Standards put a great emphasis on practice, on the application of mathematical content material to imagined or real-life situations. This doesn't come easily to most of our students. The habit of asking oneself "What answer do I expect?" of a practice problem has immediate consequences. It forces students to focus on the story line of the problem without which there is no expectation and no solution. It also helps them clarify, for instance, what operation needs to be performed or which number needs to be divided by which.

Many professionals in finance, investment, sales, real estate, manufacturing, commerce, agriculture, and so on use different ratios and percentages. They refer to them by names that change from one profession to another even when the mathematics are the same. These are often quick gauges of value or efficiency, and it helps if we can do fast calculations as decisions are made. My experience is that many who have their own expertise may be used to relying on specialized software most of the time even for these very simple calculations. They may be quite confused when that is not available. Expectation cannot be, all by itself, a full answer to their mathematical needs, but as part of a healthy mathematical diet, it can be a powerful problem-solving strategy in deciding what operation to perform.

7. Specific versus General

Legalese, the language of lawyers, lawmakers, and bureaucrats, has its reasons. It attempts to cover all contingencies, to make provisions for all possible circumstances and exceptions, and to eliminate all loopholes and the possibility of any misinterpretation or misapplication. As a result, it is perfectly incomprehensible, so it is written in fine print, and we hardly ever bother to read it. We sign on the dotted line that we are fully aware of all the possible dangers, including death, of the most benign medical procedure; we know that we risk our lives by just walking into a doctor's office or riding in a hospital elevator with a surgeon—or is it just that we get charged for those activities?

There is a mathematical equivalent to legalese. We recognize it when we see it: "Given two real numbers a and b with b $\neq$ 0" is a hint of what is coming. That language is used for just about the same reasons: we want to cover all possible contingencies, make provisions for all possible exceptions. So we—or our textbooks—couch the rules and regulations of mathematics and its definitions in the most general terms possible. This can make for heavy reading. It seems we value more the objective accuracy of those statements than what we can reasonably expect to see reflected in the brains of our students.

> There is a simple alternative to arcane general statements: to speak of the particular instead of the general. We can attach concepts to examples rather than generalized statements. The mind can understand the specific and, without any difficulty, sees the general through the example.

We all use the approach on a constant basis. When we use a diagram to represent a geometric figure, we are providing a specific instance as a convenient substitute for the more abstract general formulation. There is no such thing as a diagram of all triangles. In fact, one of the difficulties of drawing a good diagram in geometry is to make sure that the specific diagram we choose does not send the wrong message concerning the more general constraints that it represents, for instance by giving the impression that a triangle is isosceles when it isn't necessarily so. We use the specific instead of the more general when we introduce a concept by imagining a practical situation that students are familiar with. We use the approach when teaching operations on signed numbers by explaining the rules in terms of integers and then taking it almost for granted that students will very naturally broaden their understanding to real numbers and fractions.

I am writing with readers in mind and a concern for being understood and accessible, so I systematically use this approach in this book. It makes it easier to read and also much easier to write.

When, at some point, I want to show different ways of thinking about a fraction, I do not express those options in terms of fractions in general. I arbitrarily choose 3/4 and say this:

- 3/4 is another way of writing 3 ÷ 4.
- 3/4 is the quotient of the operation 3 ÷ 4.
- 3/4 is a number, a point on the number line equivalent to 0.75.
- 3/4 is 3 of something called a quarter or fourth.
- 3/4 is a ratio corresponding to 75 percent, a proportion equivalent to 3 out of 4.

"3/4 is 3 of something called a quarter or fourth." Nobody has any problem generalizing to any other fraction: "7/15 is 7 of something called a fifteenth." But how would we express that important understanding in general terms? Try it. Send me your version using the words "numerator" and "denominator" instead of specific numbers. At best, it will be longer and not as easy to understand. Then put yourself in the position of a sixth grader. It's not the truth that I formulate in its all-inclusive accuracy that matters; it's what remains in the minds of our students.

Official standards are most often, by their very nature, general statements. They are used by professionals speaking to other professionals. When I hear the standard of the day read aloud at the onset of a class, sometimes by a student with poor reading skills, using words that are not yet understood because that's going to be the lesson of the day, I think, "Okay, we've already lost the interest and attention of those students we most want not to leave behind." In the very first minutes of the class period, by speaking what can only be gibberish to them, we taught our students that it is okay not to understand, that it's okay to tune out and let spoken words flow by as in a dream. Some students may never snap out of that dream during the rest of the period. The action was adult driven, not done because we sincerely believed it was in the best interest of our students. I heard a group of teachers discuss that issue and complain that the requirement of writing down the standard of the day on the board at the beginning of the class was imposed from above and prevented them from using a gradual discovery as a central feature of their teaching strategy. One teacher had a creative solution. She said, "I write the standard where it can't be missed from the door but where students are unlikely to see it after they settle down."

One benefit of the new Common Core State Standards is that they make no pretense at speaking the language of students. Can we imagine writing on the board of a third-grade class or reading to them this standard of the day?

3.OA.2. Interpret whole-number quotients of whole numbers, e.g., interpret $56 \div 8$ as the number of objects in each share when 56 objects are partitioned equally into 8 shares, or as a number of shares when 56 objects are partitioned into equal shares of 8 objects each.

For example, describe a context in which a number of shares or a number of groups can be expressed as $56 \div 8$.

Teachers also, as they read this standard, might want to rely more on the specific of the example given in the last sentence than on the more general statement that precedes it.

8. Stories

Modeling, as described and encouraged in the standards for practice, implements what is the ultimate purpose of mathematics: the use of its tools and structures to reflect back on the real world and help us make sense of it. Stories are part of that interaction but in the opposite direction. Instead of using math to enlighten us about the world, stories allow us to use concrete illustrations from the outside world, real or imagined, to enlighten us about the more abstract processes of mathematics. They are part of the constant back-and-forth teachers routinely use between the formulations of abstract mathematics and the practical illustrations and applications that use numbers in context. Stories, like other strategies we use as we seek to teach to intuition, are mostly very simple and familiar tools used to some degree by all teachers. Here, we just want to emphasize how brief short stories or story lines of one kind or another can be woven into the fabric of mathematical explanations.

We essentially used a story line when we asked three questions to introduce addition and subtraction of fractions. We introduced a point that could be explained in purely mathematical terms by involving students in a reflection on adding cats and dogs. We established the connection between understanding and the internal logic implemented by the mathematics of fractions first on the level of imaginary but very plausible and familiar situations. We then transferred what we discovered in terms of cats and dogs to denominators.

Earlier, we initiated a conversation about shoppers at the checkout counter. Here again a story line, an imaginary rendition of a very familiar experience, led to a reflection on some of the properties of operations and the order of operations. We recognized the freedom that we have to move numbers around in a series of additions and subtractions as a familiar experience. We justified the need to multiply before we add or subtract through the story line in ways that are not apparent in the purely mathematical injunction.

At some point, we used the distributive property to find the product of two binomials. Even in the summarized version justified by the context, we felt compelled to give a human face to the process by imagining a teacher distributing 5 colored pencils and 7 sheets of paper to two classrooms of 10 and 12 students. This was not done after the fact as a possible application of the property to the real world but as part of the process of introducing the concept and the mathematics. The abstract and the practical strengthen each other. One generalizes what the other anchors in experience.

We also discussed taking away a negative: $- (-3) = 3$. At first sight, it may seem strange to our students that an overabundance of negative signs ends up as a positive number. Relying on a memorized statement such as "Two negatives make a positive" is also fraught with dangers and is bound to be applied by some where it shouldn't be. Stories are an obvious way of revealing the logic and necessity of this fact. Let me suggest a few, told interactively to the class. I am letting the reader imagine the students' side of the exchange.

- What does the offensive line do when an umpire cancels a 10-yard penalty?
  You're telling me that the line moves forward 10 yards if the umpire cancels the penalty? Does the quarterback like that?
  Canceling a penalty is like taking away a negative. It's a big plus.
- Does your teacher ever make a mistake when correcting your tests?
  Is an answer ever marked wrong when you had the right answer?
  Tell me what happens when the teacher agrees to change the grade.
  The "mistake" that you didn't make cost you 5 points. It was a negative. At first, you had 85 points on your test. What's your grade after the teacher corrects the error? Do you like that? Does it feel good when you can get rid of a negative?
- Have you ever woken up in the morning with a pimple on your nose? Never? Good. You're lucky. If you did, does that improve your good looks? You have the perfect cream to have the pimple go away. That's two negatives: the pimple, a negative, goes away—a second

negative. Do you look better after it's gone, or do you look twice as bad? In real life, as in mathematics, taking away a negative is a positive.

- Your mom: Why did you buy this shirt?
  You: Well, you can't say that it doesn't look good on me, can you?

"You can't say that it doesn't"—that's what the English teacher calls a double negative. Instead of two negatives, you could use one positive. You could say, "Well, I thought it really looked good on me."

A number of short stories—often suggested by students—spread over time can change what could be a strange rule of mathematics into something that makes sense, into something that is essentially obvious and intuitive and remains so throughout a student's academic career and beyond.

At every opportunity, we can use brief references or allusions to such stories as five-second-review material. We are building in our students' minds a connection with common sense and experience as an alternative to relying exclusively on a rule.

Let me add an actual example of a story used in a high school setting.

One Story Deserves Another

A student was at the board, taking part in an explanation of the math involved in calculating the standard deviation of a series of numbers. I had probably given some quick explanation of the concept, such as "Think of it as the average deviation from the average" or "It tells you if the data are closely bunched up around the average or more widely spread out"—all valid formulations but so abstract! It became clear that this was not enough. I needed to let the math wait and focus on the concept.

So I improvised a story.

> Imagine that the first astronauts are on their way to Mars. They've been told not to worry about Martians. Our intelligence services tell us that the average Martian is only 4 feet 2 inches tall and, size for size, they are about as strong as humans. So our strong astronauts are confident that they have nothing to fear.

> After a year-and-a-half trip, they arrive on the planet. They soon realize that they have been given the correct information: Martians average about 4 feet 2 inches. But there is a problem. Some Martians are just 1 inch tall and others measure 10 or 11 feet. The control room down on earth sends back a message: "Sorry, folks. We didn't think of that."

> Just knowing the average height wasn't enough in those circumstances. That's where knowing the standard deviation would help. The Martians' average height was 4 feet 2 inches but the standard deviation was 4 feet, which means that about one third of the Martians were either smaller than 2 inches or taller than 8 feet 2 inches.
>
> The standard deviation is a little bit like "give or take": the Martians were 4 feet 2 inches tall, give or take 4 feet!

The story aims to give immediacy to the concept, to drive home the need for it. But in this case, the student at the board soon upstaged me. She had her own story to tell.

"It's funny that you should mention astronauts going to Mars," she said. "Right now, there is a spaceship going to Mars with a rover on board. If everything goes well, in a few weeks, that little rover will be running around on Martian soil."

She then spoke about the rover. She told us its name: Sojourner. She explained how it had been named after Sojourner Truth, an escaped slave who had written about her life as a slave and her escape and who participated in the emancipation movement before the Civil War. In conclusion, the student said, "And that rover, Sojourner, she's my sister!"

That deserved an explanation. She told us her mother had been working on that project for NASA for many years. The little rover was always around as she grew up. Her mom had divided her attention between the rover and her, and she had always thought of Sojourner as her sister.

A few weeks later, as Sojourner made its historic first rounds on the planet, her mother was on TV, giving background information and updates.

In Conclusion

Thank you, reader, for accompanying me on this journey. Let's take a quick look back.

We started by learning from shoppers at a supermarket. We concluded with simple stories. In between, we offered detailed strategies on two of the more intractable hurdles of basic mathematics: We allowed cats and dogs to teach us about fractions. We used bubbles to help us make sense of integers. We also followed a spider up and down a waterspout. We explored the structure of the four operations. We tried to find alternatives to just pure memorization as we looked at the use of formulas in geometry. We briefly considered alternatives to endless drilling as students learn essential math facts. We explored strategies to help students with word problems. We appreciated the Common Core State Standards' insistence on understanding and on using mathematical knowledge to model the world in which we live. We were bold enough to make suggestions on how they could do this even more efficiently. In a variety of ways, we sought to reach our students' intuitive sense of understanding and to develop strategies for doing so that could apply beyond the topics selected here as illustrations.

In our introduction, we referred to leaders in all fields of life who see in the current level of mathematical knowledge an existential threat to the future economic well-being and international standing of the nation. It may seem absurd to put teaching about fractions, integers, math facts, and word problems in the same context as these weighty considerations, and yet, the urgency they imply is a constant backdrop as we consider even the small details of the strategies presented here. Why else make changes, significant or insignificant, to familiar practices? Those concerns reflect gaps that are real and that, in the final analysis, measure realities that exist only in the brains of our students. They reflect facts and processes that are not known, but that is only the manifestation of a deeper deficiency. What teaching to intuition seeks to address is a widespread estrangement from mathematics itself. We try to do so by an approach that has nothing to do with "dumbing down." Allowing students to connect the facts and procedures of mathematics to the intuitive patterns of their understanding is quite the opposite.

It is possible for teachers to be overwhelmed by the considerable number of issues essentially beyond our control as math teachers that impact our students' ability to learn mathematics—from the level of language proficiency to the number of students in a class, from a hearty breakfast to a place to do homework, from regular exercise to a good night's sleep, from parent involvement and expectations to the attention deficits or hyperactivity of children, from teaching art and music to the availability of a preschool experience. All these are real and need to be addressed. But as a teacher, I want to claim teaching as what by far has the greatest impact. Elementary and middle school teachers have the privilege of being those most specifically entrusted with conveying to our children the specialized mathematical knowledge that all citizens should possess. That is why we focus here on elementary and middle school material.

I belong to an association called SACNAS, the Society for the Advancement of Chicanos and Native Americans in Science. Each year, SACNAS holds a national convention where over three thousand mostly Hispanic and Native American university students— undergraduates, graduates, PhD candidates, and postdoctoral students in various scientific disciplines— have the opportunity to meet, present their research, find mentors, hear speakers on the challenges and opportunities that exist in diverse fields of science, and explore new avenues and venues for their efforts. The major universities and government agencies are there to encourage and recruit talent. It is for a talk at one of those conferences that I began to put down on paper what is now *Teaching to Intuition*.

At the same time as being an uplifting experience, it is also a sobering one. I remember the director of SACNAS at the time giving the statistics that less than 10% of Hispanics made is successfully through high school algebra. The needs of the nation for medical doctors, chemists, biologists, astronomers, geologists, engineers, high-tech experts and entrepreneurs, researchers, university professors, and high school teachers will not be met unless the pool of students from the Hispanic community able and willing to become those professionals is vastly expanded beyond those dismal statistics. That is, in very concrete terms, an example of the gaps that must be filled.

However much I would like to believe that the specific strategies on specific topics proposed here could by themselves meet the need and the urgency, I do not, and clearly, they do not. The approach we struggle to define and illustrate in *Teaching to Intuition* will only succeed if elementary and middle school teachers allow their diverse experiences and creativity to bear on it, improve on it, and expand it beyond the examples and strategies presented here. I see this attempt as contributing to the discussion and rethinking of the way we do things that must accompany the introduction of the Common Core State Standards.

We still have a long way to go.